THE
HISTORY OF
CENTRAL AMERICA

THE
HISTORY OF
CENTRAL AMERICA

Thomas L. Pearcy

The Greenwood Histories of the Modern Nations
Frank W. Thackeray and John E. Findling, Series Editors

Greenwood Press
Westport, Connecticut • London

Library of Congress Cataloging-in-Publication Data

Pearcy, Thomas L., 1960–
 The history of Central America / Thomas L. Pearcy.
  p. cm. — (The Greenwood histories of the modern nations, ISSN 1096-2905)
 Includes bibliographical references and index.
 ISBN 0–313–32293–7
  1. Central America—History. I. Title. II. Series.
 F1436.P38 2006
 972.8—dc22 2005026169

British Library Cataloguing in Publication Data is available.

Library of Congress Catalog Card Number: 2005026169
ISBN: 0–313–32293–7
ISSN: 1096–2905

First published in 2006

Greenwood Press, 88 Post Road West, Westport, CT 06881
An imprint of Greenwood Publishing Group, Inc.
www.greenwood.com

Printed in the United States of America

The paper used in this book complies with the
Permanent Paper Standard issued by the National
Information Standards Organization (Z39.48–1984).

10 9 8 7 6 5 4 3 2 1

Contents

Series Foreword

The *Greenwood Histories of the Modern Nations* series is intended to provide students and interested laypeople with up-to-date, concise, and analytical histories of many of the nations of the contemporary world. Not since the 1960s has there been a systematic attempt to publish a series of national histories, and, as editors, we believe that this series will prove to be a valuable contribution to our understanding of other countries in our increasingly interdependent world.

More than 30 years ago, at the end of the 1960s, the cold war was an accepted reality of global politics, the process of decolonization was still in progress, the idea of a unified Europe with a single currency was unheard of, the United States was mired in a war in Vietnam, and the economic boom in Asia was still years in the future. Richard Nixon was president of the United States, Mao Tse-tung (not yet Mao Zedong) ruled China, Leonid Brezhnev guided the Soviet Union, and Harold Wilson was prime minister of the United Kingdom. Authoritarian dictators still ruled most of Latin America, the Middle East was reeling in the wake of the Six-Day War, and Shah Reza Pahlavi was at the height of his power in Iran. Clearly, the last 30 years have been witness to a great deal of historical change, and it is to this change that this series is primarily addressed.

With the help of a distinguished advisory board, we have selected nations whose political, economic, and social affairs mark them as among the most important in the waning years of the twentieth century, and for each nation we have found an author who is recognized as a specialist in the history of that nation. These authors have worked most cooperatively with us and with Greenwood Press to produce volumes that reflect current research on their nations and that are interesting and informative to their prospective readers.

The importance of a series such as this cannot be underestimated. As a superpower whose influence is felt all over the world, the United States can claim a "special" relationship with almost every other nation. Yet many Americans know very little about the histories of the nations with which the United States relates. How did they get to be the way they are? What kind of political systems have evolved there? What kind of influence do they have in their own region? What are the dominant political, religious, and cultural forces that move their leaders? These and many other questions are answered in the volumes of this series.

The authors who have contributed to this series have written comprehensive histories of their nations, dating back to prehistoric times in some cases. Each of them, however, has devoted a significant portion of the book to events of the last 30 years because the modern era has contributed the most to contemporary issues that have an impact on U.S. policy. Authors have made an effort to be as up-to-date as possible so that readers can benefit from the most recent scholarship and a narrative that includes recent events.

In addition to the historical narrative, each volume in this series contains an introductory overview of the country's geography, political institutions, economic structure, and cultural attributes. This is designed to give readers a picture of the nation as it exists in the contemporary world. Each volume also contains additional chapters that add interesting and useful detail to the historical narrative. One chapter is a thorough chronology of important historical events, making it easy for readers to follow the flow of a particular nation's history. Another chapter features biographical sketches of the nation's most important figures to humanize some of the individuals who have contributed to the historical development of their nation. Each volume also contains a comprehensive bibliography, so that those readers whose interest has been sparked may find out more about the nation and its history. Finally, there is a carefully prepared topic and person index.

Readers of these volumes will find them fascinating to read and useful in understanding the contemporary world and the nations that compose it. As series editors, it is our hope that this series will contribute to a heightened sense of global understanding as we embark on a new century.

Frank W. Thackeray and John E. Findling
Indiana University Southeast

Timeline of Historical Events

8000–4000 B.C.E.	Archaic period, when Central Americans began using specialized tools, etc.
1500–600 B.C.E.	Olmec flourish and decline (Mexico); the first noted sedentary civilization in Mesoamerica
500 B.C.E.–500 C.E.	Toltec culture (Mexico) developed and flourished around capital of Monte Albán, rivaling the grandeur of Teotihuacán
300–900 C.E.	Classical Maya flourish in Yucatán and beyond
100–600 C.E.	Teotihuacán city-state (Mexico) flourished, a principal trading partner of the Maya
900–1519 C.E.	Classical Mesoamerican civilizations dissolve; postclassical era, which Spaniards encounter when they arrive in 1519
1000–1200 C.E.	Toltec flourish

1501	Rodrigo de Bastidas sets foot on Panama's Darien Coast, becoming first European in Central America
1502	Christopher Columbus explores the Central American coast on his fourth voyage
1511	Two shipwreck survivors, Gonzálo Guerrero and Gerónimo de Aguilar, wash ashore in Yucatán
1513	Vasco Núñez de Balboa "discovers" the Pacific Ocean
1517	King of Spain authorizes African slavery as a way of ending Indian enslavement
1519	Pedrarias established Panama City, the oldest European settlement on the Pacific Coast of the Americas
1527	Spanish Crown establishes Captaincies General in Guatemala and Nicaragua
1528	Pedrarias proposes canal across Nicaragua instead of Panama
1535	Bartolomé de Las Casas arrives in Nicaragua, establishes Dominican convent
1541	Santiago de Guatemala destroyed by an earthquake and the flood it triggered
1545	San Salvador is permanently established on present site
1561	Juan de Cavallón leads first successful settlers into Costa Rica
1563	Central American territory divided administratively between Panama (South American) and New Spain (everything north of Panama)
1630	British loggers begin working along the Central American coast

1660	José de Pineda Ibarra establishes first printing press in Central America
1662	Dutch begin settling along Nicaraguan coast
1671	Panama City destroyed by Henry Morgan; city moved seven miles to current site
1698–1699	Unsuccessful effort to establish Dutch settlement in Panama's Darien region
1736	San José, Costa Rica established
1739	War of Jenkins's Ear; interloper Edward Vernon attacks, destroys Portobelo
1755	British build fort at Belize
1767	Jesuits expelled from the Americas
1773	Earthquake destroys Santiago de Guatemala, which is moved to its present site in 1776
1821	Central America gains independence from Spain; Panama becomes part of Gran Colombia; remainder of Central America forms part of independent Mexico
1823	Central America declares independence from Mexico (July 1); forms United Provinces of Central America
1827–1829	Honduran Francisco Morán leads bloody civil war in Honduras, becomes leader of Central American Federation
1840	Central American Federation dissolves and independent republics emerge. Having captured Guatemala City, peasant caudillo Rafael Carrera achieves political dominance throughout the region
1843	British establish Mosquito Coast protectorate, staging ground for later gunboat diplomacy

1846	Mallarino-Bidlack Treaty guaranteed U.S. rights over Panama transit route
1850	Clayton-Bulwer Treaty confirmed British-U.S. cooperation for any canal built across Central America
1855	Panama Railroad completed and begins service
1856	"Watermelon Riot"—160 U.S. troops invade Panama, marking first U.S. military intervention in Central America
1855–1856	William Walker arrives in Nicaragua, becomes president
1860	William Walker captured, executed
1863	Belize formally becomes British colony
1870s	Liberal dictatorships arise, promoting Western economic values at gunpoint
1881–1889	French canal company tries unsuccessfully to dig canal across Panama
1894	Last British intervention on Mosquito Coast, which becomes part of Nicaragua
1899–1903	Fighting in Colombia's "Thousand Days War" spreads to Panama, leading to its independence from Colombia
1901	Abrogation of Hay-Pauncefote Treaty leaves United States free to build Panama Canal unilaterally
1903–1904	Panama declares independence from Colombia; United States begins digging canal
1907–1931	Meléndez family dominates El Salvador's economy and government
1912–1933	U.S. military forces occupy Nicaragua

1931	Panama's "Generation of '31" ousts conservative president Florencio Arosemena
1924–1936	Costa Rica dominated by conservative presidents
1928–1934	Augusto César Sandino leads Nicaraguan nationalists against U.S. occupation army; Anastasio Somoza kills Sandino, controls National Guard, becomes president
1932	Military dictatorship of General Maximiliano Hernández Martínez slaughters 30,000 peasants who were in the way of economic development (January). Known today as La Matanza, this event widens gap between the rich and poor in El Salvador
1931–1944	Jorge Ubico and Maximiliano Hernández Martínez preside over violent conservative dictatorships in Guatemala
1932–1948	Tiburcio Carías Andino's conservative dictatorship rules Honduras
1948–1958	José Figueres leads successful uprising against Costa Rica's government, then carries out social changes
1945–1954	Presidents Juan José Arévalo and Jacobo Arbenz enact social reforms in Guatemala until Arbenz's ouster in 1954
1954	George Price's liberal People's United Party wins in Belize, begins era of reform
1955	Strongman President José Remón of Panama is assassinated in a gangland-style execution
1956	Anastasio Somoza is assassinated; his sons continue family dynasty until 1979

1961   Guatemalan and Nicaraguan govern-
                ments support Bay of Pigs invasion

1961   Hurricane Hattie wrecks Belize City,
                forcing relocation of that capital

1961   Violent conservative military regimes
                dominate politics, economics in El
                Salvador

1964   Two dozen Panamanian students killed
                when American troops open fire on their
                protest; Panama severs diplomatic rela-
                tions with Washington to protest these
                murders

1964   British Honduras achieves limited self-
                rule

1969   Brief war between Honduras and
                El Salvador becomes known as the
                "Football War"

1972   Earthquake devastates Managua,
                strengthens Somoza family's hold on
                power

1973   British Honduras's name officially
                changed to Belize

1974   Hurricane Fifi devastates Honduran
                coast

1976   Earthquake devastates central
                Guatemala, tremors felt in El Salvador,
                Honduras

1977   United Nations ratifies Belize indepen-
                dence

1977   Archbishop Oscar Romero boycotts
                inauguration of military regime in El
                Salvador

1977   President Carter links military aid to
                human rights observance; Guatemala
                rejects ploy

1977	United States and Panama sign Panama Canal treaties
1977	Military government in El Salvador passes Law for the Defense and Guarantee of Public Order, eliminating restrictions on military violence against civilians in that nation
1979	Full-scale Sandinista revolution begins against Nicaragua's ruling Somoza regime, forcing Somoza's resignation July 17
1980	Archbishop Oscar Romero is assassinated shortly after petitioning President Carter to stop sending weapons to El Salvador
1981	Panamanian strongman, General Omar Torrijos, dies in mysterious plane crash, eventually giving rise to Manuel Noriega's dictatorship
1981	Belize gains full independence within British Commonwealth September 21
1981	El Salvador's U.S.-trained Atlacatl brigade slaughters community of Mozote
1982	Boland Amendment amends 1973 War Powers Act; prohibits U.S. funds from being used to overthrow government of Nicaragua (December 8); violation of this amendment precipitates the "Irangate" crisis in Washington
1984	CIA mines Nicaraguan harbors; World Court later condemns the act as violation of international law
1986	Earthquake destroys much of San Salvador
1987	Costa Rican President Oscar Arias's peace plan is adopted by Central American countries

1988	Hurricane Joan leaves more than 200,000 persons homeless in El Salvador
1989	United States invades Panama, kills more than 2,000 persons in attempt to capture Noriega
1989	El Salvador's Atlacatl brigade murders six Jesuits at the Universidad Centroamericano
1992	Peace accords implemented in El Salvador, Nicaragua; El Salvador disbands Atlcatl brigade
1992	Indigenous Guatemalan author/activist Rigoberta Menchú wins Nobel Prize for Peace with the publication of her book, *I, Rigoberta*
1992	Manuel Noriega convicted of money laundering and drug trafficking while being held in a U.S. prison in Miami
1993	Guatemala, El Salvador, Honduras sign "Northern Triangle" pact, allowing free transit across shared borders
1996	Salvadoran death squad, FURODA, named in honor of Roberto D'Aubisson
1998	Daniel Ortega, leader of Nicaragua's FSLN, is accused by his stepdaughter, Zoilamerica Narvaez Murillo, of sexually molesting her when she was an adolescent. This further divides FSLN leadership.
1998	In Guatemala, the Recovery of Historic Memory Project (REHMI) publishes a report detailing human rights abuses in Guatemala and outlining government participation in executions
1998	Monsignor Juan José Gerardi is murdered (by brick) two days after his

	organization (REMHI) publishes its report on human rights
1999	Panama takes complete control of its canal in December; last of U.S. military personnel leave the republic
2004	The Central American Free Trade Agreement (CAFTA) is signed by the nations of Costa Rica, El Salvador, Guatemala, Honduras, Nicaragua, and the United States.
2005	The Dominican Republic is added to the CAFTA, which will now be called CAFTA-DR

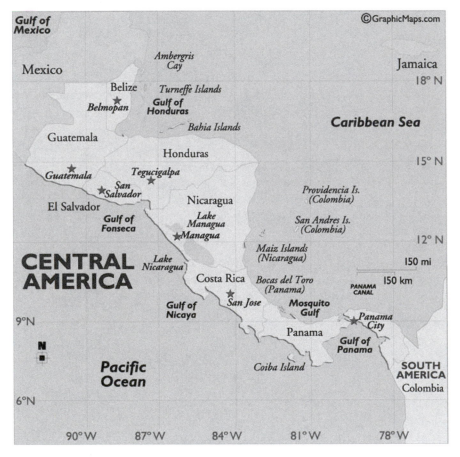

Map provided by www.worldatlas.com.

1

Introduction to the Seven Nations of Central America

The seven republics of Central America present a study in diversity. As demonstrated by Table 1.1, these countries vary considerably in size, population, and demographic characteristics. Some have roots deep in the Spanish Empire, whereas others derive their heritage from British colonizers. Dozens of indigenous languages are found in the region, but six of the seven republics have Spanish as their principal language and one nation is English-speaking. All of the republics export tropical goods and earn millions of dollars from tourism. The peoples of each nation have to deal on a regular basis with natural disasters that have the potential to fundamentally disrupt their lives.

Along with the many distinctive characteristics of the Central American nations, the end of the twentieth century brought with it a series of challenges that have forced Central American leaders to make sweeping changes that affect the very core of how each nation functions. The end of the cold war stopped decades of military and financial assistance in many of the Central American nations, which now must make difficult decisions between government ownership and privatization. In Panama, the government officially assumed full control of the canal in December 1999. Thousands of U.S. troops

Table 1.1   Statistical Profile of Central America (2004)

Country	Capital City	Size*	Population	Life Expectancy (years)	Tallest Peak (feet)
Belize	Belmopan	8,866	272,945	68	3,680
Costa Rica	San José	19,730	3,956,507	77	12,500
El Salvador	San Salvador	8,124	6,587,541	72	8,957
Guatemala	Guatemala	42,042	14,280,596	65	13,815
Honduras	Tegucigalpa	43,277	6,823,568	66	9,416
Nicaragua	Managua	50,464	5,359,759	70	7,998
Panamá	Panamá	29,762	3,000,463	72	11,401

* measured in square miles.

who had previously spent millions of dollars per year in Panama are gone, and the government of Panama has had to find imaginative ways to keep the canal functioning smoothly while compensating for the loss of income generated by the presence of a huge U.S. military presence. Moreover, governments and wealthy citizens who once used threat of violence to control workers and peasants must now find new, civil ways of maintaining public order.

The changes could not be more dramatic. Truth commissions have published scathing critiques of human rights violations by the former dictatorships in several of the Central American republics, which must now confront their earlier use of violence and *escuadrones de la muerte* (death squads) in the court of public opinion. This has not been an entirely successful process, nor has it always gone smoothly. Nonetheless, the process does move forward which, in the environment of Central American politics, is a remarkable achievement for the peoples of these nations. These introductory comments serve as an overview of how each country is confronting these sweeping changes.

BELIZE

Belize is unique among the nations of Central America for a variety of reasons. Its language, history, and culture all reflect its British heritage. Meanwhile, its political system has its roots in the nineteenth century, when, as subjects of the British Crown, Belizeans enjoyed the protection of the British military while remaining subject to a distant monarch. In 1862, the nation was renamed British

Honduras, a name that stood until the nation was renamed Belize in 1973. In September 1981, Belize gained its independence from Great Britain, becoming the seventh sovereign nation among the Central American republics.

According to its new constitution, Belize is a constitutional monarchy. The British Crown is Belize's "titular sovereign," a monarchy in name only. The British monarch is formally represented in Belize by a governor general. Actual power resides in Belize's elected parliament and its prime minister.

Since independence, these elected officials have taken Belize in a direction almost diametrically opposed to the other nations of Central America. Nationalists in other nations have sought to distance themselves from U.S. influence, but Belize has moved to strengthen its ties to the United States. Belize's foreign policy in the 1980s and 1990s proclaimed itself "non-aligned" with Britain and other countries, while reaffirming its growing "special relationship" with the United States. During the last two decades of the twentieth century, millions of U.S. dollars flooded into Belize through government agencies such as the U.S. Agency for International Development (AID.), the Peace Corps, and the Chamber of Commerce and Industry. Some critics denounced the increasing presence of U.S. citizens, cash, and influence in Belize. They contended that Belize had merely cast off one colonial taskmaster (England) to make room for another (the United States). Seen in this light, the increasing U.S. presence jeopardized Belize's independence and sovereignty much as Great Britain had before 1981.

Belize at a Glance

Population

In 2004, Belize had a population of 272, 945. The largest ethnic group in Belize is *mestizo* (mixed Indian and European ancestry), which accounts for 49 percent of the population. English is the official language, and 94 percent of the population is literate. Fifty percent of the nation is Catholic. Belizeans have an average life expectancy of 67 years.

Belizeans generally refrain from identifying themselves strictly within an ethnic group, preferring instead to call themselves Belizeans. Marriage among the various groups is common, and religion, language, and cultural traditions cut across ethnic lines, giving Belize significant cultural pluralism and ethnic diversity.

Physical Characteristics

Belize is about the size of Massachusetts, consisting of 14,270 square miles of land, 2.5 percent of which is arable. Belize is the only Central American country with no coastline on the Pacific Ocean. The highest point in Belize is Victoria Peak, which rises 3,680 feet above sea level. It borders Mexico and Guatemala and has a 240-mile coastline.

Belize has a very hot, humid tropical climate year-round. It has two seasons—the wet season (May to November) and the dry season (February to May).

System of Government

Belize's government is a parliamentary democracy, with its capital in Belmopan. Its independence day is September 21, commemorating Belize's independence from England on September 21, 1981. Belize has universal suffrage for all its citizens ages 18 and older. Its government consists of three branches: the prime minister, a bicameral national assembly, and a supreme court.

Belize does not elect its prime ministers; instead, the prime minister—who is head of government—is appointed by the governor general, who is appointed by the Queen of England. Belize's current prime minister is the Honorable Said Wilbert Musa, appointed to this position August 28, 1998. There are no term limits for Belize's prime ministers.

Economy

Belize's primary source of income is tourism. Its principal exports are sugar cane, marine products, bananas, and garments. The United States is its largest trading partner, accounting for 39 percent of its exports and 42 percent of its imports. Belize has 303 miles of paved highways and 1,481 miles of unpaved highways.

COSTA RICA

Like Belize, Costa Rica is unusual among Central American nations. While civil wars and unrest tore apart other Central American countries during much of the twentieth century, Costa Rica remained calm and comparatively stable. Costa Ricans are fiercely proud of their country's democratic government and its respect for human rights. No death squads have roamed the streets of the capital city of San José, and Costa Rica officially disbanded its military in December 1948. The absence of a military has helped ensure that no military officer can overthrow the government and establish a military dictatorship as happened in Panama and elsewhere.

How have Costa Ricans created a stable government? How have they succeeded where other governments in the region fail frequently and miserably? Costa Rica's success at sustaining its democratic way of life can be attributed to a small –but significant set of factors: extraordinary educational opportunities for its population, a strong and satisfied middle class, and excellent social indicators—high literacy rates, low infant mortality rates, and long life expectancy. Considered collectively, these characteristics have made Costa Rican society a remarkably calm, safe, and stable place to live and do business.

Costa Rica's relative stability and its highly educated population make it an attractive place for foreign companies to do business. In recent years a number of large multinational corporations have relocated portions of their operations to Costa Rica, including Intel Corporation, Proctor & Gamble, Abbott Laboratories, and Baxter Healthcare, and a host of other, smaller companies. Money generated by the presence of these companies, coupled with a thriving tourism industry and a stable export sector, helps keep unemployment low and ensures that Costa Ricans have access to reliable public services. Costa Rica's economic and political strength have given it considerable economic and diplomatic influence. In 1994, Costa Rica signed a bilateral trade agreement with Mexico, and it has since negotiated similar trade agreements with Canada, Chile, the Dominican Republic, Panama, Trinidad, and Tobago. In 1998, Costa Rica joined a Trade and Investment Council with the other Central American countries and the United States. More recently Costa Rica has pushed for a U.S.-Central American Free Trade Agreement (CAFTA). CAFTA could result in further privatization and increased foreign investment in Costa Rica and the other Central American republics.

Costa Rica at a Glance

Population

In July 2004, Costa Rica had a population of 3,956,507. Its largest ethnic group is white (including *mestizos*), which account for

94 percent of the population. Spanish is the official language, and 94 percent of the population is literate. Seventy-six percent of the nation is Catholic. Costa Ricans have an average life expectancy of 76 years.

Physical Characteristics

Costa Rica is nearly the same size as West Virginia, consisting of 31,752 square miles of land, 4.4 percent of which is arable. The highest point in Costa Rica is Cerro Chirripo, which rises to an altitude of 12,500 feet above sea level. The country borders Nicaragua in the north, Panama in the south, the Caribbean on the east coast, and the Pacific Ocean on the west coast.

Costa Rica's climate is tropical and has two seasons—the dry season (December to April) and the rainy season (May to November).

System of Government

Costa Rica is a democratic republic, with its capital in San José. Its independence day is September 15, 1821 (from Spain). Costa Rica has universal and compulsory suffrage for all citizens over 18 years old. Costa Rica's government consists of three branches: the executive, a unicameral legislative assembly, and a supreme court.

Costa Rican presidents serve four-year terms. The country has no regular military forces. Its Ministry of Public Security is charged with maintaining national security.

Economy

Costa Rica's primary sources of income are tourism, agriculture, and electronics exports. Costa Rica has 4,906 miles of paved highways and 17,395 miles of unpaved highway. The United States is Costa Rica's largest trading partner, accounting for 14 percent of its exports and 23 percent of its imports.

EL SALVADOR

Unlike in Belize and Costa Rica, rampant political violence and terror characterized life in El Salvador throughout much of the last half of the twentieth century. In 1931, El Salvador's military overthrew its civilian government and established a military stronghold on government that lasted for more than five decades. In 1932, Communist activists killed approximately 30 civilian and military personnel, and in response Martínez's forces indiscriminately slaughtered more than 20,000 civilians in an event known in Salvadoran history as *la matanza*.

La matanza made clear the lengths to which the military and the landed elite would go to repress political opposition. This violence continued for decades, culminating in the 1970s and 1980s, when the government and its death squads killed tens of thousands of people—most notably Archbishop Oscar Romero. The civil war that lasted throughout the remainder of the 1980s and into the 1990s caused death and destruction on a massive scale, killing thousands of civilians and destroying entire communities and making foreigners wary of venturing into the country for any reason.

At long last, life in El Salvador began to change substantially after the signing of a peace accord in 1992 wherein government forces and insurgent rebels agreed to put down their weapons and use the political processes instead of war to settle their differences. This peace accord caused a surge in investor confidence and, consequently, increased private investment, which has helped El Salvador's economy to begin growing again. One of the keys to this private investment has been the privatization of much of El Salvador's economy. Industries previously owned and controlled by the government are now being sold to private investors, who in turn are making them more competitive and diverse.[1]

El Salvador desperately needs privatization and economic diversification to work. Until recently, coffee had been the backbone of the Salvadoran economy, much as it had been since the nineteenth century. World coffee prices have declined so precipitously in recent years, however, that El Salvador's exports have declined disastrously. In 1988, coffee accounted for more than 50 percent of El Salvador's total exports, but by 2004, it accounted for only 7 percent. Without the economic diversification created by privatization, El Salvador would today be facing the same catastrophic situation it faced in the 1930s.

Now, instead of violently repressing peasants while trying to wait out the abysmal coffee market, Salvadorans have diversified into a number of new industries that are compensating for the lost coffee revenue. For example, the nation's textile industry has expanded and created thousands of new jobs while generating millions of dollars in exports. These textile exports go largely to the United States, which consumes nearly 70 percent of El Salvador's exports. In December 2004, El Salvador became the first nation to ratify the Central American Free Trade Agreement (CAFTA), which will guarantee preferential access to the United States for Salvadoran textiles and other manufactured goods. Failure of the other countries to ratify the CAFTA could have catastrophic effects on El Salvador—a nation caught between the need to diversify its economy while finding a secure market for goods produced as a result of this diversification. Perhaps more than any other Central American nation, El Salvador's future remains questionable and its well-being intrinsically linked to the other countries of Central America and to the United States.

The nation's history suggests that El Salvador's wealthy are not prepared to simply sit back and watch their fortunes erode. Fortunately, privatization and increased foreign investments may offer an alternative. If not, the world may yet witness a repeat of the slaughters that characterized Salvadoran history throughout the tragic, long twentieth century.

El Salvador at a Glance

Population

In July 2004, El Salvador had a population of 6,587,541 person.Its largest ethnic group, *mestizo*, accounts for 90 percent of the population. Spanish is the official language, and 80 percent of the population is literate. Eighty-three percent of the nation is Catholic. Salvadorans have an average life expectancy of 71 years.

Physical Characteristics

El Salvador is slightly smaller than Massachusetts, consisting of 13,073 square miles of land, 32 percent of which is arable. The highest point in El Salvador is Cerro El Pital, which rises to an altitude of 8,957 feet above sea level. El Salvador borders Guatemala in the north and Honduras in the south.

El Salvador is the smallest country in Central America and the only one without a Caribbean coastline. Its climate is tropical and has two seasons—the dry season (November to April) and the rainy season (May to October).

System of Government

El Salvador is a republic, with its capital in San Salvador. Its independence day is September 15, 1821 (from Spain). It has universal suffrage for all citizens more than 18 years old. El Salvador's government consists of three branches: executive, a unicameral legislative assembly, and a supreme court.

Salvadoran presidents serve six-year terms. El Salvador has compulsory service in its armed forces for persons age 18, and each soldier is required to serve one year in the military. Individuals between 16 and 17 years old may enlist.

Economy

El Salvador's primary sources of income are tourism, agriculture, and electronics exports. It uses the U.S. dollar as its official currency. Its most important agricultural crops are coffee, sugar, and bananas. El Salvador has 1,234 miles of paved highways and 4,997 miles of unpaved highways.

The United States is El Salvador's largest trading partner, accounting for 68 percent of its exports and 50 percent of its imports.

GUATEMALA

When the United States helped Carlos Castillo Armas overthrow the government of Jacobo Arbenz Guzman in 1954, it helped start a civil war that claimed more than 200,000 lives over the next five decades. After the overthrow of Arbenz's civilian government, Guatemala's presidency became a proverbial revolving door of military dictatorships intent on eliminating communist influence in their nation. The pinnacle of this bloody civil war was the presidency of retired General Efrain Rios Montt, who, at the time of his 1982 inauguration, was a lay minister in the evangelical protestant Church of the Word. In his inaugural address, Rios Montt announced that his ascension to the presidency had been the "will of God," and he acted as if he were divinely appointed. He annulled the nation's constitution, disbanded its legislature, suspended political parties, and cancelled electoral law.

These sweeping, dictatorial steps served as an accurate prelude of the remainder of Rios Montt's presidency. In July 1982, he announced to a gathering of Guatemalan Indians that, "If you are with us, we'll feed you; if not, we'll kill you." He meant what he said. His presidency marked the most violent period in the civil war that followed the 1954 overthrow of Jacobo Arbenz. Rios Montt practiced "scorched earth" policy against Guatemala's indigenous majority, using the Guatemalan military to systematically eliminate entire indigenous communities—a plan that bordered on genocide (purposefully murdering members of a specific ethnic or racial group). During Rios Montt's administration, tens of thousands of Guatemalans died, and many thousands of others became homeless, landless political refugees. In the late 1990s, when human rights groups could finally investigate government brutality in Guatemala, they found that government forces had been responsible for more than 90 percent of the human rights abuses that occurred during the decades-long war.

Guatemala finally began its gradual shift away from state-sponsored terrorism with the 1986 election of a civilian president, Vinico Cerezo. President Cerezo moved the country away from human rights abuses while attempting to establish the rule of law to replace the vigilante justice that had plagued Guatemala under the military dictatorships. Cerezo successfully withstood two attempted military revolts (1988, 1989), a clear signal that Guatemalans were rejecting their violent history in favor of civilian rule.

In 1990, another civilian, Jorge Cerrano, won the presidency. This was modern Guatemala's first transition from one democratically elected civilian government to another. The move toward peace and civilian rule culminated in December 1996, when another civilian president, Alvaro Arzu, brokered a peace accord that officially ended Guatemala's decades-old civil war. Arzu and his successors turned their attention to improving relations with Mexico, the United States, and the other nations of Central America. Arzu and his successors sought to improve Guatemala's image abroad to attract foreign investment, a first step toward privatization and other changes needed to jump-start Guatemala's economy.

Despite the remarkable progress made in Guatemala during the return to civilian rule in the 1990s, the country continues to struggle through its own identity crisis. On the one hand, successive civilian regimes have sought to strip the military of its governmental influence, yet on the other hand human rights activists, judicial workers, journalists, and witnesses in human rights trials continue to be intimidated—sometimes violently—by insurgents opposed to the openness required for democratic reform. In 2001, the government called for national dialogue on challenges facing the country, but after four years little progress has been made on this front.

Unlike other Central American countries where reforms have advanced sufficiently to facilitate investment and economic diversification, Guatemala must continue to make progress if it is to remain under civilian rule. Unlike El Salvador, for example, Guatemala is a couple of years away from being ready to fully participate in the Central American Common Market (CACM). At some point in the future, however, the common market could be decisive in helping ensure that Guatemala does not return to brutal military repression.

Guatemala at a Glance

Population

In July 2004, Guatemala had a population of 14,280,596. More than half of its population is descended from the indigenous Mayan people. Its largest ethnic group is *mestizo*, a combination of Indian and European, which constitutes 55 percent of the population. Indians (in this case Maya) account for 43 percent of the population. Spanish, the official language, is spoken by 60 percent of the population. Indian languages are the main language of 40 percent of the population (this includes 23 officially recognized Indian languages), and 70.6 percent of the population is literate. Six years of education are compulsory in Guatemala. The nation's predominant religion is Catholicism, although many Guatemalans practice Indian indigenous religions. Guatemalans have an average life expectancy of 65 years.

Physical Characteristics

Guatemala is the largest and most populous nation in Central America. It is about the same size as Tennessee, consisting of 42,042 square miles of land, 13 percent of which is arable. The highest point in Guatemala is Volcan Tajumulco, which rises to an altitude of 13,815 feet above sea level. It borders Mexico, Honduras, Belize, and El Salvador, the North Pacific on its west coast and the Gulf of Honduras (Caribbean) on its east coast. Despite its coast, Guatemala has no natural harbor on its west coast.

Guatemala's climate is tropical. Its warmest regions are on the coast, and its milder climate is in the highlands.

System of Government

Guatemala is a constitutional democratic republic, with its capital in Guatemala City. Its independence day is September 15, 1821 (from Spain). Guatemala has universal suffrage for all citizens over 18 years old except for military soldiers, who may not vote and on election day are confined to barracks. Guatemala's government consists of three branches: executive, a unicameral Congress of the Republic, and a constitutional court.

Guatemala's presidents are elected to four-year terms. The country has compulsory military service for all males 18 years old. The term of service is 30 months.

Economy

Guatemala's primary source of income is agriculture, which accounts for more than 80 percent of its gross national product. Coffee, sugar, and bananas are its main export products. Income distribution is highly uneven, with 75 percent of the population living in poverty. Its official currency is the *quetzal*, though the U.S. dollar also circulates widely. The United States is Guatemala's largest trading partner, accounting for 57 percent of its exports and 34 percent of its imports.

HONDURAS

From 1932 to 1949, the military dictatorship of General Tiburcio Carías Andino governed Honduras with an iron fist. Carías was quite willing to use violence to subjugate political opponents and maintain order. His dictatorship created a legacy of military intervention in the nation's political processes that far outlasted Carías's government. Between 1949 and 1963, civilian politicians competed with military officers for control of the nation's government. This competition ended in October 1963, when the military toppled the civilian government and installed a new president, General López Arellano. Thus began a series of military dictatorships that endured in one form or another until 1981.

During the 1960s and 1970s, a series of border skirmishes between Honduras and its neighbors caused the Honduran military to undertake an accelerated program of modernization aimed at making it able to repulse invading enemy forces. In July 1969, Honduras and El Salvador fought a brief –but deadly border war known as the Soccer War. Honduras's modernized air force quickly proved too much for the beleaguered Salvadorans, destroying nearly all of El Salvador's tiny air force. In the late 1970s and the early 1980s, the civil war in Nicaragua once again challenged Honduras's ability to defend its borders. Incursions from both sides of the Honduras/Nicaragua border resulted in many firefights and thousands of deaths on both sides.

Honduras's border with Nicaragua also drew the United States into the region. U.S. officials hoped to bolster anti-Communist forces and help topple the Communist Sandinista regime that came to power in Managua in 1979. Throughout much of the next decade, the United States used Honduras as a staging lane from which to launch attacks on sites inside Nicaragua, helping to weaken the Communist presence in the region.

Honduras was the vanguard of those nations returning to civilian rule after decades of military dictatorships. Amazingly, at the height of unrest and chaos in El Salvador, Honduras, and Nicaragua, in the early 1980s, Honduras began making significant progress toward civilian rule. In November 1981, the nation held general elections; and in 1982, the government enacted a new constitution, one that hinged on civilian rule. President Roberto Suazo Córdoba aligned himself with the United States, which funneled millions of dollars into the Honduran economy. This infusion of currency enabled Suazo to begin gradual public works projects, and the presence of U.S. agencies, such as the Peace Corps and US AID staff assisted him as he undertook to provide fresh drinking water, roads, electricity, and other services to more of the Honduran people. Additionally, Suazo courted and received huge sums of U.S. military assistance and hardware, which helped him offset the instability caused by the raging civil wars in El Salvador and Honduras.

In January 1998, President Roberto Flores Facusse took office, the fifth consecutive civilian president to do so since the democratic reforms of 1981–1982. Later that year, Flores confronted a problem far more devastating than the civil wars of the 1980s: Hurricane Mitch came ashore in Honduras, killing 5,000 Hondurans and leaving 1.5 million people homeless. Hurricane Mitch caused in excess of $3 billion in damages to a nation that could not absorb such complete devastation. President Flores established a transparent process through which his government handled more than $600 million in foreign aid. Flores' government received international praise for its handling of the disaster and the open, equitable distribution of cash assistance.

Perhaps the most remarkable fact regarding the effects of Hurricane Mitch in Honduras is that during and after the crisis, the military never stepped in to overthrow the government and exploit the tragedy. Flores served out his term, and in 2001, Ricardo Maduro Joest won the presidential election, becoming Honduras's sixth consecutive civilian chief of state. Maduro worked hard to continue strengthening Honduras' financial situation. He also strengthened Honduras's ties with the United States: Following the U.S. invasion of Iraq in March 2003, Honduras sent 370 of its troops to Iraq to support the U.S. presence there.

As occurred in El Salvador, Honduras' transition to civilian rule has led to economic diversification. Beginning shortly after Suazo's election, Honduras began exporting new products in an attempt to diversify its economy. The effort has been a success: Honduras now exports melons, shrimp, and textiles while hosting an ever-increasing tourist industry that pumps millions of dollars into its economy. When coffee prices declined sharply in the 1990s, Honduras's economy shifted its focus to these other exportable goods, surviving the coffee crisis and creating new possibilities in a work force whose well-being had always depended on the merciless ebb –and flow of the world's coffee markets.

President Maduro became one of the principal promoters of CAFTA. Like El Salvador, Honduras is at a moment in its history when its economy may receive much-needed revenue and access to a huge market if CAFTA is approved. Like El Salvador, Honduras stands to benefit from the access to markets and much-needed revenue made possible by CAFTA. And like El Salvador, CAFTA may be the surest way to prevent Honduras from returning to a brutal military dictatorship.

Honduras at a Glance

Population

In July 2004, Honduras had a population of 6,823,568. Its largest ethnic group is *mestizo* (combination of Indian and European), which account for 90 percent of the population. Spanish is the official language, and 76.2 percent of the population is literate. Ninety-seven percent of the nation is Catholic. Hondurans have an average life expectancy of 66 years.

Physical Characteristics

Honduras is slightly larger than Tennessee, consisting of 69,649 square miles of land, 10 percent of which is arable. The highest point in Honduras is Cerro Las Minas, which rises to an altitude of 9,416 feet above sea level. It borders Guatemala, El Salvador, and Nicaragua. Honduras has a small Pacific Coast but a long Caribbean shoreline, including the largely uninhabited Mosquito Coast.

Honduras's climate is subtropical in the lowlands and temperate in the highlands.

System of Government

Honduras is a democratic constitutional republic, with its capital in Tegucigalpa. Its independence day is September 15, 1821 (from Spain). Honduras has universal and compulsory suffrage for all citizens over 18 years old. Honduras's government consists of three branches: executive, a unicameral National Congress, and a supreme court.

Honduran presidents are elected by popular vote to four-year terms. Honduras has a volunteer army, and one must be 18 years old to enlist.

Economy

Honduras is one of the poorest countries in the Western Hemisphere, with radically unequal distribution of income. Its unemployment rate was 28 percent in mid-2004. Honduras's principal source of income is agriculture, most notably bananas, coffee, and citrus products. It has 1,724 miles of paved highways and 6,728 miles of unpaved highways. The United States is Honduras's largest trading partner, accounting for 66 percent of its exports and 53 percent of its imports.

NICARAGUA

In 1933, Anastasio Somoza García became head of Nicaragua's National Guard, an armed unit established by the United States to maintain order once American troops withdrew from that nation. By 1936, Somoza had made himself president of the republic, an office he controlled until his assassination in 1956. By controlling both the presidency and the National Guard, Somoza manipulated the nation's government and its economy to his benefit while using the National Guard to terrorize his opponents into submission. After Somoza's death in 1956, his son Luis Somoza Debayle succeeded him in office. In June 1967, Luis died of a heart attack and his brother, Anastasio "Tachito" Somoza Debayle, assumed the presidency and control of the National Guard.

As his term drew to its conclusion in 1971, the dictator merely amended the constitution to enable him to remain in office. With absolute control of the National Guard, there was little constraining Somoza to consider the good of the nation. This became most apparent in December 1972, when a devastating earthquake destroyed approximately 80 percent of the capital city of Managua, killed 10,000 people, and left 50,000 homeless. Amazingly, in the wake of the quake the National Guard joined in the looting of businesses, and Somoza stole tens of millions of dollars of international aid meant to help the nation recover. Some estimates suggest that Somoza's personal wealth increased by $400 million in the 18 months after the earthquake. Somoza's greed and disregard for human suffering stunned the international community; it also deeply angered Nicaraguans who had suffered immeasurable hardships at Somoza's hands. The nation was ripe for change.

In 1961, a small group of students and intellectuals formed the *Frente Sandinista de Liberación Nacional* (the Sandinista National Liberation Front, or FSLN, also known as *Sandinistas*) to oppose the Somoza dictatorship. Initially, the FSLN remained mostly underground in order to survive, occasionally getting arrested and put in jail when they ventured into the public realm. By the 1970s, however, the FSLN had garnered the support of peasants and even a few moderate businessmen opposed to the dictatorship. Angered by what they witnessed in the months after the 1972 earthquake, the FSLN became increasingly strident in its opposition of the Somoza government. In December 1974, a group of Sandinistas took several ranking members of the government hostage and demanded a huge ransom, which they ultimately received. Infuriated, Somoza declared war on the Sandinistas, launching a series of violent offensives against the Sandinistas and their supporters.

This exchange between the FSLN and the Somoza government effectively began a civil war that raged off and on for the next five years. Tachito Somoza used a wide variety of military hardware against the rebels, eventually leveling entire towns in an attempt to defeat the insurgency once and for all. The insurgents endured, however, and on July 17, 1979, Somoza resigned and fled the country. He took refuge in Paraguay, where he was assassinated on September 17, 1980 when leftist guerillas blew up his armored car.

On July 19, 1979, the Sandinistas and their allies entered Managua victorious and in charge of a new government. Their war with Somoza had killed approximately 50,000 people and left hundreds of thousands homeless. They inherited a country torn by civil war, an economy that was nearly destroyed and was deeply in debt, and a population that had suffered decades of despotic abuse at the hands of the Somoza family. Of the various groups that had opposed Somoza, the Communist FSLN soon emerged as the dominant and decisive force in the new Nicaraguan state.

Daniel Ortega emerged from the leadership of the FSLN to take charge of the new government, and he quickly aligned Nicaragua with the Soviet Union and Cuba. With the support of these two countries, Nicaragua had an army of 80,000 troops in the mid-1980s. The weapons and training they received from the USSR and Cuba made the Sandinista army the best, most well-armed army in all of Central America.

Communism in Nicaragua proved to be a curious thing. Daniel Ortega and the other Sandinistas certainly improved literacy, life expectancy, and access to education, medicine, and so forth; however, the Communists always believed they enjoyed the popular support of the people. When opponents demanded free and open elections in 1989, Ortega agreed, believing he would win an overwhelming victory that might quiet his critics. Under close international supervision, Nicaragua held a presidential election in February 1990. To the astonishment of the FSLN, they lost the election and the presidency to Violetta Chamorro, widow of a popular newspaper publisher who had been murdered by Somoza in 1978. The stunned young Communists peacefully left office, seemingly bewildered as to how they might have been voted out of office by popular election. Ortega has been a candidate in each of Nicaragua's four presidential elections since his defeat in 1989; each time he has lost by a large margin.

Since the end of the Sandinista revolution in February 1990, Nicaragua has made great strides toward putting its economy back together. The nation's presidents have cut Nicaragua's foreign debt in half while reducing inflation from 13,500 percent to 5.3 percent. Meanwhile, the government has privatized more than 350 formerly state-owned businesses while taking steps to attract foreign investors, and foreign investment continues to increase in areas such as communications, energy, and manufacturing. Like the economies of other Central American countries, Nicaragua's economy is primarily agricultural, but more recently diversification to include textiles, gold, seafood, and a host of agricultural products (melons, peanuts, sesame, onion, etc) has alleviated some of the problems caused by the shrinking coffee economy.

Nicaragua at a Glance

Population

In July 2004, Nicaragua had a population of 5,359,759. Its largest ethnic group is *mestizos* (mixed Indian and European), which accounts for 69 percent of the population. Spanish is the official language, and 68 percent of the population is literate. Eighty-five percent of the nation is Catholic. Nicaraguans have an average life expectancy of 70 years.

Physical Characteristics

Nicaragua is about the same size as the state of New York, consisting of 80,463 square miles of land, 16 percent of which is arable. The highest point in Nicaragua is Mogoton, which rises to an altitude of 7,998 feet above sea level. It borders Costa Rica and Honduras, with extensive coasts on both the Pacific Ocean and the Caribbean Sea.

Nicaragua's climate is tropical in the lowlands (especially along the coasts) and temperate at higher elevations.

System of Government

Nicaragua is a republic, with its capital in Managua. Its independence day is September 15, 1821 (from Spain). Costa Rica has universal suffrage for all citizens at least 16 years old. Costa Rica's government consists of three branches: executive, a unicameral national assembly, and a supreme court.

Nicaraguan presidents serve five-year terms. It has a volunteer army for persons 17 years and older.

Economy

Nicaragua is another of the Western Hemisphere's poorest nations. It has a highly inequitable distribution of wealth, a huge external debt, and an unemployment rate greater than 22 percent. Nicaragua's primary source of income is agricultural exports, including coffee and bananas, though it also exports some shrimp. Nicaragua has 1,301 miles of paved highways and 10,524 miles of unpaved highway. The United States is Nicaragua's largest trading partner, accounting for 36 percent of its exports and 25 percent of its imports.

PANAMA

In January 1964, U.S. troops shot and killed two dozen Panamanian high school and university students during a confrontation over the flag of Panama. More than any other event in Panama's history, this single mass murder forced Panama to demand a rethinking of the Panama Canal treaties. It also forced the United States to begin gradually relinquishing control of this vaunted waterway. The events of January 9, 1964 fundamentally altered relations between the two countries.

The 1960s were a turbulent time in Panama, as students clashed with the government and anti-Americanism reached fever pitch. These crises culminated in October 1968, with a military revolt that ousted President Arnulfo Arias and established a military dictatorship in Panama that would last until December 1989.

After a brief internal struggle within the National Guard, General Omar Torrijos emerged as its commander, and thus, the controlling force in the new government. As he settled into power, Torrijos appointed a "provisional president" who provided a façade of democracy, but from early in the process, Torrijos remained the driving force behind the new government. Then, in October 1972, Torrijos assumed the role of chief of state under the titles of Head of Government, and Maximum Leader of the Panamanian Revolution. In this capacity Torrijos enacted a new constitution and sweeping new labor laws in addition to inaugurating progressive new programs in education, health care, and assistance for the poor. With these reforms and changes, Torrijos established a broad-based coalition and enjoyed considerable support from Panamanians, particularly rural Panamanians.

Opposition to Torrijos' policies and aggression was kept in check by a vigilant National Guard and by nationalism (anti-Americanism in this case), the proverbial glue that held together diverse sectors of Panamanian society. As long as Torrijos spoke publicly and frequently about taking control of the canal and forcing U.S. citizens out of Panama, he was assured a broad following that included many people who otherwise opposed him. In 1974, U.S. Secretary of State Henry Kissinger had begun negotiating a new canal treaty with his Panamanian counterpart, Juan Antonio Tack. Watergate scuttled these efforts, however, and they were not resumed until President Carter was elected in 1976.

The culmination of Torrijos's efforts (and the dreams of many Panamanians who deeply resented the huge U.S. presence) was the Torrijos-Carter treaties of 1977, officially known as the Panama Canal treaties. On September 7, 1977 Torrijos and Carter met in Washington and signed these historic treaties, one of which ensured U.S. control until 1999 and one of which ensured U.S. rights to defend the canal after 1999 should its well-being be endangered.

The treaties were the last great accomplishment of General Torrijos. Before the treaties were signed, Torrijos's opponents had hesitated to challenge him publicly. They needed him to continue to press the United States on the canal issue. After the consummation of this treaty, however, Torrijos opted to resign his post as head of state in 1978, permitting, instead, a civilian president to govern. Despite the opportunistic opposition that emerged in 1978 and thereafter, Torrijos remained a national hero for Panamanians who believed that he restored Panama's dignity in the international community. On July 31, 1981, General Omar Torrijos died in a mysterious plane crash that has not yet been adequately explained. His death left a huge void in Panama and throughout Central America, where as a statesman he had the prestige to moderate civil wars and perhaps help negotiate peace.

Torrijos's untimely death triggered a power struggle within the National Guard. After two years of posturing, General Manuel Antonio Noriega emerged as the Supreme Commander of the National Guard (which he renamed the Fuerzas de Defensa de

Panamá—the Panama Defense Forces, or PDF). Under Noriega, no politician could hold office without the support of the National Guard, and he supported a series of puppet presidents who would do as he told them. Noriega remained the decision maker in Panama's political circles, and as that nation's economy soured in the mid-1980s, he became increasingly aggressive and willing to use public violence to crush government opposition.

Noriega proved to be considerably more ruthless than Torrijos. While Torrijos's "populist" economics (spending money to gain public support) had gained him widespread support and helped stifle political opposition to his policies, Noriega used violent repression to control his political opponents. The crisis surrounding Noriega's repression culminated on October 3, 1989, when Major Moíses Giraldi and a small group of disgruntled officers attempted to overthrow him. After several hours, the revolt failed and Noriega loyalists rescued their chief, arrested Giraldi and his fellow plotters, and executed them. Two months later the United States launched "Just Cause," a military invasion of Panama aimed at capturing Noriega. After two weeks, U.S. forces finally tracked down Noriega, arrested him, and brought him to the United States to stand trial for narcotics trafficking. Noriega currently resides in a federal prison in Miami where he is serving a 30-year term for narcotics trafficking.

The December 1989 invasion of Panama ended the military dictatorship that had plagued that nation for more than two decades. Unfortunately, during the invasion, the United States secreted Guillermo Endara onto an American base in the Canal Zone and had him sworn in as president. Although Endara enjoyed considerable popular support, he forever will be labeled as an American lackey who came to power on Washington's shoulders.

Despite the label, Endara finished his term in office and was followed by another civilian, Ernesto Pérez Balladares. Pérez Balladares represented the political party, *Partido Revolucionario Democrático* (the Democratic Revolutionary Party—or PRD) which Torrijos had founded. Pérez Balladares was followed by another civilian, Mireya Moscosa, Panama's first female president. Then, in 2004, Torrijos' son, Martín Torrijos, made history when he won the presidency running as the candidate of his father's political party, the PRD.

Since Panama's violent return to civilian rule, it has successfully confronted major challenges. In 1999, President Moscosa successfully handled the transfer of the Panama Canal, and she helped ensure that Panama was prepared to undertake that monumental challenge. Her successor, Martín Torrijos, has enacted laws ensuring transparency of government while seeking to control government corruption, a problem that was rampant during the governments of Endara and Pérez Balladares.

Today, foreign investment is flooding into Panama, its financial and commerce sectors are flourishing, its canal is operating superbly, and its tourist industry is expanding (ecotourism, for example) at unprecedented rates. Panama is not party to CAFTA, but its control of the canal gives Panama access to foreign dollars not available to the other Central American nations. It faces other challenges, most notably the preservation of its rainforests to ensure that the canal will continue to function, appropriate privatization of former U.S. military holdings, and proper maintenance of the waterway. To date, the canal is more productive, with more transits, than it was during the U.S. era.

Panama at a Glance

Population

In July 2004, Panama had a population of 3,000,463. Its largest ethnic group is *mestizos* (Indian and European), which accounts for 70 percent of the population. Spanish is the official language, and 93 percent of the population is literate. Eighty-five percent of the nation is Catholic. Panamanians have an average life expectancy of 72 years.

Physical Characteristics

Panama is slightly smaller than South Carolina, consisting of 48,591 square miles, 7 percent of which is arable. The highest point in Panama is Volcán de Chiriquí, which rises to an altitude of 11,401 feet above sea level. It borders Costa Rica and Colombia, with extensive Pacific and Caribbean coastlines.

Panama's climate is tropical maritime; hot, humid, cloudy; prolonged rainy season (May to January) and a short dry season (January to May)

System of Government

Panama is a constitutional republic, with its capital in Panama City. Its independence day is November 3, 1903 (from Colombia).

Panama has universal, compulsory suffrage for all citizens 18 years and older. Panama's government consists of three branches: executive, a unicameral legislative assembly, and a Supreme Court of Justice.

Panamanian presidents serve five-year terms. A 1994 constitutional amendment abolished the nation's military.

Economy

Panama has a diversified economy that exports agricultural goods and textiles. The hub of its economy is its canal and the service sector that surrounds it. Panama is now developing its ecotourism industry. Unemployment in Panama is at nearly 14 percent.

Panama has 2,450 miles of paved highways and 4,632 miles of unpaved highway. The United States is Panama's largest export market (12.2%), but Japan is Panama's largest source of imports, accounting for 33 percent of Panama's imports.

NOTE

1. Industries affected include El Salvador's banking system, telecommunications, public pensions, electrical distribution and some electrical generation.

2

Early Central America

At first glance, Central America appears to be an idyllic place where hardy travelers can live out their "survivor" dreams while enjoying the thriving ecotourist industry. The first things visitors notice when they arrive in Central America is its rugged terrain, verdant plant life, exotic wildlife, and remarkable geographic and climatologic diversity. Along the Atlantic Coast, eastern plains and tropical vegetation make for an unforgiving environment where heat and extremes in climate make life difficult for those who live there. To the west, towering mountains and active volcanoes gently descend to the Pacific Coast, where fertile volcanic soils and a comparatively mild climate provide a more hospitable environment for the region's inhabitants. Between the coasts, cavernous valleys weave among the towering slopes, making travel possible among the highlands, plains, and coasts.

First glimpses can be deceiving. As those who live there know, Central America's unparalleled beauty can also be deadly. For many centuries its geographic and climatologic extremes have shaped the way people live, work, and travel in Central America. In addition to extremes in its tropical climate, Central America has more active volcanoes than any other stretch of land on the planet.

Long before the arrival of the first Europeans in 1501, Native Americans moved frequently among the valleys, hills, plains, and rain forests in search of sustenance and protection from the elements. Ancient Central American agricultural techniques required them to move around frequently in search of nutrient-rich soils and streams where they would have a dependable supply of water. While dealing with the realities of day-to-day survival, early Americans also had to contend with natural disasters and other hardships caused by the Isthmus's central location in an evolving capitalist economy wherein access to raw materials and markets would figure decisively in Central America's future after the arrival of Europeans in the New World.

NATURAL DISASTERS

Located along what geologists refer to as the "Ring of Fire," Central America has in excess of 100 volcanoes, including more than a dozen that are active. The small Cocos tectonic plate, where Central America is located, converges with the much larger Caribbean and North American plates. Over the centuries, frequent activity along these points of convergence has resulted in earthquakes and occasional volcanic eruptions, and the region's inhabitants have always lived under the specter of devastation and death because of this tectonic activity.

For centuries before the advent of Europeans in the Americas, the Maya and other groups native to the region struggled to survive amid volcanic and earthquake activity. An Aztec codex (an ancient system of writing on deer skin or paper) noted the first recorded volcanic eruption in the Americas, Popocatepetl, in 1345. To the south, one Mayan deity, Caprakán ("he of two feet"), was God of the earthquakes. The Maya implored Caprakán in hopes of placating the deities and lessening the devastating effects of seismic activity. That the Maya pantheon of gods included one relating to earthquakes accentuates the fact that the earliest Americans had to deal with seismic devastation. Long before the first Europeans arrived in 1501, Central Americans lost communities and lives when the earth started to shake.

When the Europeans arrived and began building their communities they, too, had to confront the region's tectonic instability. Throughout Central America's long colonial period (1501–1821), earthquakes and volcanoes occasionally destroyed cities, killed large numbers of people, and forced indigenous people and Europeans alike to relocate in order to survive. In the 1540s, for example, Guatemala's capital city, Santiago de Guatemala (today Ciudad Vieja occupies this site), was destroyed when an earthquake breached a lake bed and sent millions of gallons of water rushing down the mountainside, destroying the city. In 1610, Spanish authorities actually moved the Nicaraguan city of León to escape further destruction by earthquake. In 1773, an earthquake once again destroyed Santiago de Guatemala, and three years later officials there decided to move the capital city 30 miles away to avoid further destruction.

This devastation continued throughout the twentieth century. In 1902, Guatemala's 12,361-foot Santa María erupted in a spectacular explosion—one of the largest eruptions of the entire twentieth century. The cloud of ash reached 18 miles high, and the explosion was heard and felt in Costa Rica, 500 miles away. This massive explosion obliterated one side of the mountain and created a crater three-fourths of a mile wide, nearly one mile long, and 1,500 feet deep. Witnesses reported that ashes covered more than 125,000 square miles, and the 2,500-square miles surrounding the volcano became covered with more than eight inches of pumice stone and ash. This eruption crushed many houses and buildings, causing total destruction in some areas and killing approximately 6,000 people. Santa María erupted again briefly in 1929, causing significant disruption, though not as much as during the 1902 eruption.

El Salvador also experienced volcanic devastation in the twentieth century. A small country, El Salvador is Central America's most volcanically active region. Along its coast is the volcanic cone called Izalco, one of the most active volcanoes in the world. Mariners navigate by its near-constant lava flow, which from a distance appears as a magnificent incandescent flare. Izalco was unknown until 1770, when it formed in the midst of a flat cattle ranch. That year, an earthquake shook the earth and a crater appeared, spewing an enormous amount of steam, lava, and other materials. Since 1770, more than 50 additional eruptions have piled up enormous quantities of materials, now forming a volcano in excess of 6,000 feet where a flat cattle pasture had once existed. Known to mariners as *El Faro del Pacífico* (the Lighthouse of the Pacific) because of its frequent colorful eruptions, Izalco last erupted in 1966.

Table 2.1 Twentieth-Century Earthquakes

Year	Country	Deaths	Size of Quake
1902	Guatemala	2,000	7.5
1931	Nicaragua	2,400	5.6
1972	Nicaragua	10,000	6.2
1976	Guatemala	23,000	7.5
1986	El Salvador	1,000+	5.5

Earthquakes and volcanic activity occasionally still cause cata-strophic damage in Central America (see Table 2.1). In March 1931, an earthquake measuring 5.6 on the Richter scale devastated Nicaragua's capital city of Managua. This catastrophe killed more than 2,000 people and forced the abandonment of portions of the city. Then, in December 1972, a larger quake, measuring 6.2, again struck Managua and forced officials there to relocate portions of the capital city. In February 1976, a massive earthquake measuring 7.5 struck Guatemala, killing 23,000 persons and causing extensive damage.

Central Americans have also had to live with occasional devastat-ing hurricanes that reap havoc similar to that caused by earth-quakes. Throughout the colonial period, hurricanes destroyed towns, uprooted people, and caused widespread destruction along Central America's coasts. Like earthquakes, the problem with hur-ricanes has persisted. Belize City was destroyed by hurricane Hattie in 1961, and officials opted to move the capital city inland 50 miles to Belmopan. In 1998, Hurricane Mitch, the most destructive hurri-cane to visit the region in 200 years, struck along the Atlantic Coast, devastating everything in its path. Hurricane Mitch killed thou-sands of people and caused billions of dollars in damage, leaving immense amounts of human suffering in its wake.

As seen in Table 2.2, Hurricane Mitch demonstrates just how dev-astating hurricanes can be to Central America. Unlike volcanoes, damage from Mitch was not regional—it affected entire countries. Beyond the stunning toll of dead and missing, 3 million people were left homeless, and the storm caused more than $8 billion in damages. Schools, roads, hospitals, homes, bridges, airports, agriculture— everything in the path of Mitch's sustained 180 miles –per hour winds was destroyed. Dumping between 30 and 50 inches of rain in

Table 2.2   Deadliest Hurricanes in Twentieth-Century Central America

Name of Storm	Year	Country	Dead and Missing
Mitch	October 1998	Belize, El Salvador, Guatemala, Honduras, Nicaragua	18,000+
Fifi	September 1974	Honduras	8,000–10,000
*	June 1934	El Salvador, Honduras	2,000–3,000
*	September 1931	Honduras	1,500–2,500
Gordon	November 1994	Costa Rica	1,145**

*   American forecasters began naming hurricanes in 1953.
** Death toll includes those killed by the storm in countries outside of Central America.

its path, Mitch destroyed more than 150,000 tons of grain in Honduras alone and many more tens of thousands of tons of grain elsewhere in its path.

Mitch's broad path of devastation severely strained the governments of Honduras, El Salvador, Guatemala, and Nicaragua. In Honduras, for example, President Carlos Roberto Flores Facusse handled $600 million in foreign emergency assistance while struggling to repair the nation's badly damaged infrastructure (bridges, roads, phone lines, etc.). The survival of civilian government hung in the balance, and Flores successfully pulled his nation through the catastrophe without the violent military intervention and widespread government corruption that occurred in Nicaragua after an earthquake in 1972.

Foreign Aggression

Beyond natural disasters, Central Americans have had to confront persistent assaults by foreign encroachers looking to establish a presence in the region and to exploit the area's resources. Welsh buccaneer Henry Morgan attacked Panama City in 1671, destroying it with fire and forcing the Spaniards to relocate the city five miles down the coast. In 1855, American filibusterer William Walker invaded Nicaragua and declared himself president, only to be executed by Honduran forces after causing trouble for several years. Later, foreign presence along the Nicaraguan coast gave rise to an era of gunboat diplomacy—the violent subjugation of the region by British forces. Finally, in recent decades, the specter of U.S. intervention has loomed over the Central American countries. Throughout the twentieth century, the United States sent its troops repeatedly into the region, sometimes for many years, to crush rebellion, change unfavorable governments, and occasionally to dictate courses of action. Only Costa Rica and Belize avoided having the U.S. government intervene in their nation's affairs.

Amazingly, despite the many hardships they face—earthquakes, hurricanes, volcanoes, direct foreign military intervention—the people of Central America have survived and flourished. Thus, the most noteworthy characteristic one might notice while studying Central America is the resiliency and will to survive of its people.

THE PEOPLE

Native Americans lived in Central America for millennia before prior to the arrival of Europeans. Surviving Maya architecture indicates that indigenous people Natives living in northern Central America had mastered sophisticated agricultural techniques that enabled them to live in large communities. These same ruins capture in great detail the sophistication of Mayan art, religion, commerce, and warfare. Discoveries made in the past 50 years tell the story of an extremely complex, advanced civilization that endured for centuries as an imperial power.

This chapter tells contains the story of Central America's highly complex peoples, how they lived, and how they encountered Europeans early in the sixteenth century. The complexity of Central America's peoples helps us understand why the colonial period in Central America differed so markedly from that of Mexico and South America. Guatemala's Maya, for example, struggled for nearly 200 two hundred years to resist subjugation by Europeans. In the end, Mayan capitulation in the late seventeenth century had less to do with military conquest than it did with agriculture. Spaniards took control of so much land that traditional Mayan agricultural techniques became increasingly difficult to sustain.

This resiliency during the colonial era also helps us understand Mayan resiliency in the face of the genocidal intents of Guatemalan governments during the last decades of the twentieth century. For the Maya, the "scorched-earth" war Guatemala's President Rios Montt declared against them in the 1980s was merely a continuation of a struggle that has now gone on for more than 500 five hundred years. To understand more recent events in Central America, it is necessary to understand the region's past. Only then is it possible to comprehend fully the depth of problems modern Central America faces today.

For thousands of years inhabitants of Central America moved around frequently in small, nomadic bands searching for food and shelter. Living "off the land," these peoples responded in diverse ways to the varied climatologic and geographic circumstances they encountered. Some began settling in what we would recognize today as tiny communities, and others continued in a fluid fashion to move from place to place in search of water and fertile soil as the seasons changed. As noted in Table 2.3, by the time Europeans first arrived in Central America in the early sixteenth century, the region had witnessed the rise and fall of small city-states and the great Mayan civilization, one of the three great classical civilizations in American history (Aztec, Maya, Inca).

In northern Central America, this nomadic lifestyle started to change when the Olmec civilization began to take shape as the region's first sedentary population center with a centralized, sedentary system of governance. The Olmec appeared and thrived during the period scholars refer to as the Preclassical Period, —roughly 3000–1000 B.C.E., reaching their pinnacle during the period around 1150 B.C.E. Jade and elaborate stone work characterized the Olmec at the height of their preeminence, and the most important city to emerge during the Olmec era was San Lorenzo. The most widely recognized artwork from the period are the massive basalt heads, some of which weigh many tons and are intricately carved. Evidence suggests that the Olmec maintained extensive trade relations with peoples throughout Central America, including those residing as far away as El Salvador, Nicaragua, and Costa Rica.

In southern Central America, natives settled along waterways and near the coasts to have access to fresh water and produce. No great classical civilizations arose that approached the scope and grandeur of the Maya, but prehistoric people living in what is today Panama and Costa Rica left their own indelible print on the landscape. Substantive settlements began to emerge beginning around 800 B.C.E. in Central Panama. The Central Panamanian civilization (Panama) and the Chiriquí, Atlantic Watershed, and Nicoya cultures (Costa Rica) appeared and flourished around 800 B.C.E. (Central Panama). Later cultures developed and thrived in these two countries until 1530, when the Parita Phase (Panama), Chiriquí, Cartago, and Polychrome Ceramic Cultures (Costa Rica) began to wilt under European pressure for raw materials and land.

In the area that became Panama City, natives traded with distant merchants including the great Inca Empire to the South. Evidence suggests that Inca traders visiting Panama before 1532 contracted smallpox from Europeans, carrying it with them when they returned to the Incan heartland. This epidemic decimated the Inca, killing thousands of them, weakening that great nation and paving the way for Francisco Pizarro and his band to attack in 1532.

Unknown until the late 1970s, El Caño contains the ruins of Central Panama's "Coclé Culture," which flourished between 500 A.D. and the arrival of the Europeans in the sixteenth century. El Caño has five large burial mounds, a ball court, and what many believe to be an indigenous calendar. Little is known about the people who lived at El Caño because so little money has been available for excavation and preservation. It is known, however, that they had extensive trade with other peoples, even those living many hundreds of miles away. In Belize, for example, elite burials contain gold and copper objects from Oaxaca, West Mexico, and the Veraguas region of Panama (near El Caño) in addition to quantities of local and Yucatec ceramics.

In the dry plains and rugged hills of Central Panama, indigenous populations thrived along river banks where they established communities and religious centers. Around 750 C.E., for example, a powerful chief died in Panama's central region of Coclé and was entombed at Sitio Conte on the banks of Río Grande de Coclé in central Panama. His people buried the chief with 22 sacrificed companions and a wealth of gold finery, including large pectoral plaques embossed with sacred images. This site in Coclé is the richest pre-Colombian tomb unearthed thus far in southern Central America.

Remnants left by the ancient inhabitants of Central America offer a glimpse into what life was like in pre-Colombian America. In the north, sites unearthed by archeologists reflect the grandeur of the ancient Mayan civilization. The remnants of communities large and small tell the story of advanced civilizations with complex political, religious, and agricultural systems. In southern Central America, archeologists have found smaller communities dispersed around the harsh countrysides of Panama and Costa Rica. Findings at these southern sites contain religious centers, royal burial chambers, and

Table 2.3   Ancient Civilizations of Central America

Period	Northern Central America	Mexico
7000–1800 B.C.E.	archaic cultures	
1800–1500 B.C.E.	pre-Olmec cultures	
1500–400 B.C.E.	Olmec cultures	
1800–400 B.C.E.	early and middle formative cultures (Central Mexico)	
1800–300 B.C.E.	southern Maya cultures	
1800–250	pacific preclassical (plain and highland)	
1400–500 B.C.E.	Valley of Oaxaca cultures	
1000 B.C.E.–250 C.E.	lowland preclassical culture	
1000 B.C.E.–900 C.E.		Teuchitlán traditional cultures (Western Coast)
400 B.C.E.–300 C.E.		Epi-Olmec cultures (Gulf Coast)
300 B.C.E.–250 C.E.	late preclassical cultures	
300 B.C.E.–600 C.E.	Kaminaljuyú culture (southern region)	
100–650 C.E.		Teotihuacan city-state (Central Mexico)
1–900 C.E.		Monte Albán (Southern Mexico)
250–700 C.E.	regional cultures (northern region)	
250–900 C.E.	dynastic city-states (central region)	
250–900 C.E.	Puuk culture (northern region)	
300–1000 C.E.		Regional Veracruz cultures (Gulf Coast)
600–800 C.E.	regional cultures (southern region)	
600–1150		El Tajin city-state (Gulf Coast)
650–1200 C.E.		Regional cultures (Central Mexico)
950–1000 C.E.	Toltec Culture (northern region)	
800–1200 C.E.	Mexicanized Cultures (southern region)	
900–1250 C.E.		Tarascan culture (Western Mexico)
1000–1200 C.E.	Toltec-Chichén city-state	Toltec city-state (Central Mexico)
1000–1521 C.E.		Cempoala city-state (Gulf Coast)

(Continued)

Table 2.3 (continued)

Period	Northern Central America	Mexico
1000–1521 C.E.		Mixtec and Zapotec kingdoms (Southern Mexico)
1150–1521 C.E.		Huastec cultures (Gulf Coast)
1200–1350 C.E.		Northern emigrant cultures (Central Mexico)
1200–1441 C.E.	Maya pan city-state (southern region)	
1200–1530 C.E.	K'iché and neighboring states (southern region)	
1250–1532		Tarascan State
1350–1521 C.E.		Aztec nation (Central Mexico)
1441–1527 C.E.	Regional Centers (northern region)	
1527–1535 C.E.	Conquest Period (northern region)	
1530–1542 C.E.	Conquest Period (southern region)	

	Southern Central America		
Period	Panama	Southern Costa Rica	Eastern Costa Rica	Northern Costa Rica
---	---	---	---	---
800 B.C.E.– 100 C.E.	Early Central Panamanian cultures			
200 B.C.E.– 200 C.E.		Early Greater Chiriquí cultures		
100–500 C.E.	Central Panamanian cultures		Atlantic Eatershed cultures	Greater Nicoya cultures
500–800 C.E.			La Selva- Curidabat cultures	
500–1530 C.E.				Polychrome Ceramic culture*
200–700 C.E.		Greater Chiriquí cultures		
500–800 C.E.	Conte Phase cultures			
700–1000 C.E.		Sierpe Phase cultures		
800–1000 C.E.	Macaras Phase cultures			
800–1530 C.E.			Cartago-La Cabaña cultures*	
1000–1530	Parita Phase cultures*	Chiriquí culture*	.	

stunning artwork that were left behind by complex civilizations who had mastered their surroundings.

CONTACT AND EXPLORATION, 1492–1521

During his fourth journey to the "Indies" in 1502, Christopher Columbus sailed along Central America's east coast, briefly exploring the Gulf of Honduras before sailing south to Panama. Columbus and those who came afterward encountered a region remarkably diverse in its climate, geography, and people. Over much of the next two decades, intrepid Europeans plied the waters off the coast of Central America in search of the Indies and treasure.

Unlike Mexico and South America, Central America offered little enticement for Europeans seeking wealth and glory. Instead, those who explored the region found prohibitive topography and a difficult climate that made life there insufferable. Also, Central America offered no rich caches of precious metals that would lure Europeans into the harsh countryside. Classical Mayan civilization had collapsed 600 years earlier, and the postclassical civilizations that the Spanish encountered were a mere shadow of the former grandeur of the Maya heyday. Central America in 1500 had no equivalent to Mexico's Teotihuacán or Tenochtitlán.

Exploring Panama

Sailing from Hispaniola in the years after Columbus's initial voyage in 1492, Europeans at times would have viewed the coast of Central America during their journeys. With little compelling them to explore deep into the Central American heartland, however, Europeans did not have much contact in the region in the years after Columbus's initial voyage. The first sustained effort occurred in 1501, when Rodrigo de Bastidas sailed from Hispaniola to the mouth of the Magdalena River. From there, he journeyed north to explore Panama's Gulf of Darien coastline. While exploring the gulf, Bastidas collected various artifacts, none with any compelling value or appeal. After experiencing difficulties with the indigenous population, Bastidas abandoned his exploration of the Darien region and returned to Spain via Hispaniola.

One member of Bastidas's expedition, Vasco Núñez de Balboa, returned to Panama along with explorer Francisco Pizarro, later the conqueror of the great Inca Empire. This group resumed Spain's exploration of Panama's east coast, and eventually established a community in the Darien region that thrived under Balboa's leadership. From his location in Panama's eastern rain forest, Balboa explored the harsh interior of the Isthmus. Natives told him of a "South Sea" and a place of great wealth, "Birú," the Inca Empire. In September 1513, Balboa "discovered" the "South Sea" and became the first European to see the Pacific Ocean. From there he returned to the Darien region.

In Spain, the Crown wearied of Balboa's assertive disposition and prepared to send Pedro Arias de Ávila (also known simply as Pedrarias) to replace Balboa and rein him in. As Pedrarias prepared to sail, however, word arrived of Balboa's encounter with the "South Sea," and these tales of riches caused Spanish royals to reconsider their rebuke of Balboa. Instead, the Crown forgave Balboa and named him *Adelantado* (person appointed by the Crown to explore, conquer, and secure new territories) and Captain General of the provinces of Panama and Coiba. Although Pedrarias was his superior, Balboa continued to enjoy considerable leeway and influence on the Isthmus.

Two men of considerable accomplishments and egos, Pedrarias and Balboa found it next –to impossible to remain in Panama together. Balboa resented Pedrarias, Pedrarias did not trust Balboa, and consequently the two competed aggressively with each other and struggled to coexist peaceably. This jockeying for position culminated in 1519, when Pedrarias accused Balboa of treason. After a perfunctory trial, Pedrarias found Balboa guilty and had him summarily beheaded. The "Discoverer of the South Sea" died an ignominious death at the hands of his political rival.

Contact in the North

Europeans had little substantive contact with northern Central America in the decade after Christopher Columbus's exploration of its coastline in 1502. In 1511, a Spanish ship sank while en route to Jamaica. Many of those who survived the shipwreck fell victim to militaristic Caribs. Two survivors, Gonzálo Guerrerro and Gerónimo de Aguilar, washed ashore in the Yucatán region. Guerrero thrived among his hosts, teaching them military tactics that would enable them to fend off European encroachers when they arrived. This training paid off in 1517, when Francisco Fernández de Córdoba led a military party from Cuba to explore the Yucatán. Perhaps because of techniques taught them by Guerrero, the indigenous population repelled the Europeans and forced them to retreat to Cuba before achieving a toehold on the coastline.

Unlike the loyal Guerrero, Aguilar left his Indian hosts and joined Hernán Cortés's landing party when they arrived in 1519 to begin their march to the Aztec capital of Tenochtitlán. Having learned language, customs, and geography in his years among the Natives, Aguilar proved to be a useful guide and member of the Cortés expedition. Along with the Indian woman Malinche, whom Cortés used as a linguist/guide, Aguilar provided the advancing Spaniards with the critical ability to communicate with nations along their fateful march toward Tenochtitlán.

Tracking through the rugged Yucatán toward the Central Mexican Valley, Cortés capitalized on the linguistic skills of Malinche and Aguilar to negotiate and, when necessary, fight. Many tribes the Europeans encountered deeply resented he Aztecs and welcomed the opportunity to assist Cortés in his advance on the Aztec capital of Tenochtitlán. The Spaniards and their newfound allies encountered their stiffest resistance when they happened on the Tlaxcalans—excellent warriors and avowed enemies of the Aztec. The Tlaxcalans had carried on a war of resistance against the Aztecs for many years and thus despised the inhabitants of Tenochtitlán. They resisted the newcomers, though, and fought the advancing Spaniards bitterly. In the end the Spaniards prevailed with the support of their indigenous allies, and the Tlaxcalans became Cortés's most valuable ally in his march toward the Aztec capital.

Exploration: Securing a Central American Beachhead

Further exploration of northern Central America was delayed until after Cortés and his people had conquered the Aztec and solidified their hold of the Aztec capital. After the Aztec fell, Cortés set about expanding his realm and solidifying his control of the region. The immediate issue was Pedrarias's expansion northward from Panama. If Cortés did not rein in northern Central America— Guatemala and Honduras, specifically—he risked relinquishing the area to Pedrarias.

The Maya fiercely resisted European encroachment of their homeland. Unlike the highly centralized Aztec and Inca Empires, Central America's harsh environment prevented all but the very heartiest of explorers from penetrating too deeply. Possibly using tactics taught them by Guerrero, the Maya resisted early attempts by emissaries sent by Cortés to pacify the area. Alarmed that Pedrarias was on the verge of occupying much of the region, in 1526 Cortés personally traveled overland to Honduras and there established the community of Puerto Natividad (renamed Puerto Cortés in 1869).

In the early decades of contact and exploration, Europeans regularly fought among themselves for control of New World real estate. On Florida's east coast, for example, Spaniards fought and killed dozens of French Huguenots for control of the area of St. Augustine. In the case of Central America, Spaniards fought among themselves for the right to claim the influence and control that accompanied the pacification of new territories.

Once the Europeans solidified their hold on Tenochtitlán in 1521, Cortés began making preparations to expand his reach southward and to pacify that region and secure its control. In 1523, Cortés sent his second-in-command, Pedro de Alvarado, to explore south of the Yucatán and to subdue the region's inhabitants.

In December 1523, Alvarado and a large army left Mexico City bound for Guatemala and Honduras. As fate would have it, Guatemala's Cakchiquel and Quiché tribes were fighting a civil war that had decimated both sides. As Cortés had done previously, Alvarado allied himself with one side, the Cakchiquel, and used this alliance to defeat the Quiché and subdue the area. By July 1524, Alvarado was able to establish a European capital city among the Maya, established at Iximché, the Cakchiquel capital. Over time, Iximché's location proved disadvantageous, and Alvarado's brother Jorge relocated the European city of Guatemala City to the base of Volcán Agua, the site of present-day Ciudad Vieja. Earthquake devastation would later compel Europeans to relocate the city yet again, but the European presence now permanently existed in Guatemala.

After the relocation and stabilization of Guatemala City, Pedro Alvarado spent the next two years forcibly subduing indigenous populations in Guatemala and El Salvador. He established various new permanent European communities along the way, sowing the seeds of permanent Spanish influence in his wake. In Honduras, Alvarado encountered Pedrarias's soldiers, triggering an extremely divisive boundary dispute between Alavarado and Pedrarias that lasted for several years. Then, in 1527, the Spanish Crown named Alvarado governor of Guatemala, a sweeping territory that included portions of present-day Costa Rica,

Nicaragua, El Salvador, Honduras, Guatemala, and the Mexican state of Chiapas. This decree put an end to the immediate fighting between Alvarado and Pedrarias, but it provided little permanent relief from boundary disputes. Once Francisco Pizarro began plundering Incan gold, Alvarado grew restless and abandoned his post to seek his fortune in the Andes. Incan gold would, after all, be transported to Spain via Panama, and Alvarado's successful lobbying for control of Guatemala ironically precluded him from cashing in on the Incan booty that would traverse the Isthmus of Panama. Border disputes remain a problem in Central America today, some five centuries after Pedro Alvarado and Pedrarias faced off in their now infamous border disputes.

Unlike what occurred in Mexico and the Andean highlands, Spain's subjugation of Central America proceeded slowly and in stages. Effective and total subjugation of the Maya in Guatemala did not occur until 1697. In the interim, however, the Kingdom of Guatemala served as a base of operations from which Europeans defeated and subjugated distant and restive indigenous populations of El Salvador, Honduras, Belize, and Costa Rica. Only late in the seventeenth century did Guatemala's Petén succumb to European domination. Even at that late date, the Maya evaded military defeat. Europeans increasingly isolated Guatemala's rural indigenous population by using up increasingly large amounts of precious Mayan farmlands for hemp production. Much like what occurred in the American West, the Maya of Guatemala fell victim over time to fences and foreign agricultural techniques that robbed them of precious lands and resources that had for centuries supported the *milpa*, the Maya's land-intensive slash-and-burn technique of preserving stable nitrogen levels in the region's topsoil.

3

From United Provinces to Independent States: Costa Rica, El Salvador, Guatemala, Honduras, and Nicaragua

Independence from Spain brought opportunity and hardship to all of Latin America, including Central America. In eighteenth-century Spain, a series of sweeping administrative changes known collectively as the Bourbon Reforms had liberalized Spain's administration of its American colonies. Among other things, these reforms multiplied acceptable ports of call for commerce traveling between Spain and its colonies. Previously, Panama had monolized Spain's trade with its South American colonies; the Bourbon Reforms cost Panama its vital role in Spanish commerce. Moreover, throughout the colonial period Creoles (whites born in the Americas) had been able to hold certain high offices in the colonial bureaucracy, including seats on the *audiencia*, the highest regional court in Spanish America. By preventing Creoles from holding these positions in the eighteenth century, the Bourbons effectively alienated all of their American-born subjects. By excluding American-born subjects from high offices, the Bourbons also created vacuum in leadership experience that would come back to haunt the colonies after independence. Without experienced leadership, independence plunged the Central American states into a period of administrative chaos characterized by lawlessness and rule by *caudillo* (regional political bosses that generally ruled with an iron fist).

Mexico's independence from Spain resolved little in Central America. In 1822, Mexico became a monarchy and named Agustín de Iturbide its emperor. That same year Central America annexed itself to the Mexican Empire much as Panama had annexed itself to Gran Colombia the previous year. Once again, Central Americans found themselves beholden to a distant monarch, and once again unrest engulfed Guatemala City. This alliance lasted little more than a year, however, as Iturbide's government fell and Central America declared its absolute independence from Mexico on July 1, 1823. At that point, a provisional junta established a new government to rule over the United Provinces of Central America (UPCA).

This new political entity encompassed five of Central America's seven new nations: Guatemala, Honduras, El Salvador, Nicaragua, and Costa Rica. Panama remained a part of Gran Colombia where it would continue throughout the course of the nineteenth century, and Great Britain claimed Belize from Mexico.

COSTA RICA

Long before its independence from Spain in September 1821, Costa Rica had grown into a unique state quite distinct from its Central American neighbors. Excepting Belize, the other nations in Central America are predominantly *mestizo* (a person of mixed Spanish-Indian heritage). Costa Rica, on the other hand, is predominantly European. This difference results from a variety of factors, most notably that Costa Rica had a comparatively small population of Indians when the Europeans arrived. Finding few precious metals in Costa Rica, Spaniards who settled there became farmers and small, relatively impoverished landowners.

Over the course of three centuries, Costa Rica developed a unique culture of equality among the population. Unlike colonial El Salvador and Guatemala, for example, the gap between rich and poor was narrowest in Costa Rica, where Spaniards worked the fields and tended to the needs of their families. Moreover, since it was so far from the colonial government in Guatemala, there was relatively little pressure from officials and other outsiders. There simply was little besides land to attract people. That environment held little for the adventurous Spanish *conquistador* (conqueror) soul of the colonial era.

After independence, class distinctions became slightly more pronounced in the nineteenth century as farmers began growing bananas and coffee for export; however, these exports did not affect Costa Rica as drastically as they had other Central American countries. Costa Ricans had multiple sources of income and many different ways to survive. While coffee and sugar ranchers became wealthy, Costa Rica enjoyed a unique sense of national well-being even when the coffee economy declined markedly at the end of the nineteenth century. Unlike in other nations, the financial hardships caused by declining coffee prices did not trigger political violence and military dictatorships in Costa Rica. Instead, at the height of the coffee crisis, in 1899 Costa Rica held its first open, democratic election.

The 1899 election began a tradition of democracy in Costa Rica that has been briefly interrupted only twice since 1899. Toward the end of World War I, the Costa Rican government enacted land and income taxes and proposed banking oversight regulations to help offset the economic decline caused by the war. In response to this government intervention, the coffee oligarchy encouraged General Federico Tinoco to step in as a military dictator, which lasted for two years. Then, José Figueres led an armed uprising in the wake of the disputed 1948 election. Figueres's uprising triggered a 44-day civil war that killed 2,000 people, easily the bloodiest, most violent event in modern Costa Rican history. Figueres was later democratically elected in his own right.

EL SALVADOR

In the early history of the republic of El Salvador, liberalism took on a distinctly economic flavor. As world demand for indigo slowed precipitously, the enormous profits generated by that industry gave El Salvador's landed elite the ability to move aggressively into the coffee industry, which by the mid-nineteenth century dominated the nation's economy. By 1871, these wealthy Salvadorans had established the "coffee republic," referring to the total dominance of coffee in El Salvador's economy. This one-crop "coffee republic" lasted until the beginning of the Great Depression in the late 1920s.

El Salvador's wealthy did well by investing so fully in coffee. Between 1880 and 1914, the value of coffee exports rose more than 1,100 percent. During this same period, coffee provided nearly 60 percent of government revenue. Whether or not the nation's coffee barons occupied the nation's presidency, the wealth they contributed to the federal government gave them incredible influence in El Salvador's halls of power. Wealthy Salvadorans controlled the nation's government and its military.

The influence of wealthy coffee families became most apparent in 1912, when the government founded the nation's *Guardia Nacional* (National Guard). While the nation's National Police was charged with keeping order and enforcing the nation's laws, the *Guardia Nacional* was established specifically to protect coffee *fincas* (farms). Many of the larger *fincas* had their own *Guardia* posts located directly on the grounds of the coffee estate, and this institutionalized repression of rural unrest was reaffirmed when the *finca* owner would reward regional *Guardia* officers with money and gifts. In this way, the nation's coffee-growing elite, represented by the ubiquitous *Asociacion Cafetalera* (Coffee Growers Association), became known as the "invisible government" of the country.

The "Coffee Republic" did well until the outset of the Great Depression, when coffee export prices declined 54 percent. In an attempt to preserve their own profits, landowners lowered farm worker salaries by 54 percent or more. Food supplies declined drastically, and the suffering of the nation's rural poor intensified rapidly. Desperate rural peasants came to listen increasingly to radicals such as Agustín Farabundo Martí, a Marxist agitator who espoused radical change at the expense of the nation's wealthy.

Throughout 1931, the rural poor regularly protested their living and working conditions and clamored for change. The elite and the military opposed making any concessions to these workers, and yet conditions showed no signs of improvement; the nation's depressed coffee economy made for increased unemployment, lower wages, and more difficult living conditions generally. Thus throughout late 1931, the rural poor repeatedly protested the inequalities of life in the Salvadoran countryside.

Further complicating El Salvador's political situation was the election of a reform-minded candidate, Arturo Araujo. Araujo had established his own labor party modeled on the British system, which made the nation's elite very uncomfortable. After his election, Araujo ran into a number of severe problems, the combination of which captures the essence of Salvadoran history since the early 1930s: civil servants wanted higher pay, peasants wanted land reform, and the oligarchy and military demanded that Araujo give no such concessions.

Araujo's flirtation with liberal reforms deeply concerned El Salvador's wealthy, which had no intention of allowing the new president to make any moves that would jeopardize the nation's social and economic hierarchies. On December 21, they could wait no longer, and a military coup drove Araujo from power. General Maximiliano Hernández Martínez assumed the presidency, and he had no intention of allowing liberal reforms or in any way acquiescing to peasant demands.

Excluded so thoroughly from power in this way, peasant insurgents decided to revolt in guerilla-like uprisings in various small communities throughout El Salvador's coffee country. Organized by the leader of El Salvador's Communist Party, the flamboyant Martí, this peasant army hoped to bring El Salvador's economy to a halt and force the government to acquiesce to their demands. Martí planned for the uprising to occur January 22, 1932, but the military learned of the uprising in advance and captured Martí and several of his colleagues and incarcerated them.

The nominal peasant leadership that remained tried to call off the uprising, but word spread slowly and on January 22, the revolt began without Martí's decisive leadership. The peasants killed several merchants and landowners, but in the end their machetes had little effect against the army's modern weapons, which had come largely from the United States to fight "communism." The military quickly retook cities lost to the peasants and completely crushed the rebellion. El Salvador's governing elite and its military wanted revenge. The military systematically hunted down peasants who had participated in the January 22 uprising, branded them "Communists," and executed them. This massacre, known in Spanish as *La Matanza* (the slaughter), killed approximately 30,000 peasants.

The military executed Martí and a few of his co-conspirators February 1, 1932. This execution at the hands of the military forever made Martí an iconic figure in the politics of El Salvador. Today, the *Frente Farabundo Martí para la Liberación Nacional* (Farabundo Martí Front for National Liberation—or the FMLN) in El Salvador invokes his name while pursuing a leftist agenda.

The events of December 1931-January 1932 marked a critical turning point in twentieth-century Salvadoran history. Frightened by the violence of the uprising, El Salvador's tiny economic elite reached an agreement with the nation's military that has had enduring consequences for that nation: the oligarchy would unilaterally control the nation's economy, and the military would control its government. Over time this combination proved decisive as ranking officers frequently shared a portion of the oligarchy's wealth in exchange for special service—ranging from extra personal protection to arranging death squads to eliminate political or economic enemies.[1]

GUATEMALA

Precious little changed after independence for those living in northernmost Central America. Before the collapse of the Spanish Empire, foreigners set up a system of government where a numerically small minority governed the indigenous majority—frequently at gunpoint. After independence, relations between indigenous populations and foreigners continued to be a point of friction. Governments used vagrancy laws and a host of other administrative tools to subjugate indigenous populations and retain control of their raw materials.

As had been the case with the federalist–anti-federalist debate in the United States, the relationship between state governments and federal authority sparked unrest and civil war. Liberals advocated the separation of church and state, the confiscation of church property, immigration from Europe, and the development of an economic infrastructure that could promote the increase of imports and exports—frequently using land grants to encourage Europeans to immigrate to Guatemala. For 15 years after the establishment of the Central American Union, liberals and conservatives fought a bitter civil war that jeopardized the stability of the entire region. In the late 1820s and early 1830s, the war grew so divisive that Spanish loyalists actually gained control of the Honduran city of Omoa.

These early conflicts between liberals and conservatives culminated in the 1830s with the administration of Mariano Gálvez, Chief of State in Guatemala from 1831 to 1838. Gálvez launched a series of sweeping anticlerical and economically liberal reforms aimed at expanding demand for Guatemala exports abroad while increasing the foreign investment in Guatemala City.

As Chief of State in Guatemala, Gálvez led the push for liberal reform in the new nation. The head of the Central American Confederation during the same period, Francisco Morazán, pushed for similar measures throughout the entire UPCA. Morazán, a military general from Honduras, had become president of the UPCA in 1829. On the federal level, he promulgated the same liberal platform that Gálvez promoted inside Guatemala. Morazán's policies proved as divisive as Gálvez's program. liberal reform alienated rural populations where religion figured prominently. They also alienated the region's large indigenous population, whose labor and wealth lay at the core of liberal economic designs.

Over time a sizable anti-liberal insurgency arose from among the masses throughout the United Provinces of Central America. The principal leader of this counterinsurgency was Rafael Carrera, a ladino of Spanish, Native, and African lineage. Born in Guatemala City in 1814, Carrera received no formal education and worked at odd jobs until the mid-1830s. In 1836 and 1837, a cholera epidemic seized much of Guatemala, and many peasants attributed this as divine retribution caused by the liberal reforms enacted by Gálvez and Morazán. Coupled with the anxiety and hardships caused by the reforms themselves, the cholera outbreak triggered a widespread revolt that came to be known as the War of the Mountain. The war quickly spread throughout the entire region, covering an area from Costa Rica to Quetzaltenango (western Guatemalan highlands). The uprising spread at a stunning pace. Throughout much of the Central American heartland, Carrera's forces quickly expanded to include Indians, ladinos, mulattoes, and zomobos. This large alliance of popular groups challenged the governing urban white Creoles and Europeans who favored liberalism.

This war starkly reflected the fundamental differences between liberals and conservatives throughout all of Central America. Liberals favored a republic, free trade, and close control of the church. Conversely, conservatives favored a monarchy, restoration of the Catholic church to a position of preeminence, and trade controlled more closely by Spain. Over the course of the long colonial era, the church in many rural areas had championed the cause of the poor in the face of liberals seeking to exploit them. An attack on the church reflected an attack on the region's large, impoverished rural population. Carrera had little difficulty mustering support for his anti-liberal insurgency.

The universality of unrest expressed itself in the failure of the UPCA. In 1838, Nicaragua, Honduras, and Costa Rica seceded from the UPCA, effectively dissolving the union. Guatemala seceded in 1839, and El Salvador followed suit in 1840, bringing an end to the union and ushering in the modern era in Central

American history, characterized by separate republics with quite distinct agendas and allegiances.

Carrera's war against liberalism epitomized the struggle between conservatives and liberals in the post-independence era, and support for him expanded quickly and easily. By early 1838, he had defeated Gálvez's forces and driven him from office. With effective control of government in Guatemala City, Carrera's forces began reversing the liberal reforms they so opposed: they restored the church to its place of former prominence, removed military governments, and called for a return to constitutional rule. Carrera couched his actions in populist language that appealed to the masses. He announced, for example, that he would restore laws and personal liberties while reversing the many changes liberals had made that impinged on the region's poor.

As events in Guatemala unfolded, UPCA leadership took desperate steps to crush Carrera's guerilla army. With secession unfolding throughout the region, at stake in Guatemala was nothing less than the UPCA's continued existence. Morazán's assault on Carrera's forces marked the definitive early clash between liberals and conservatives to occur in postindependence Central America. Marching at the head of 1,000 federal troops from El Salvador, Morazán's federal army launched an all-out assault on the insurgents. Carrera's forces responded ferociously, attacking the advancing federal army and taking aim particularly at foreign-owned properties. To Carrera's peasant army, foreign-owned businesses epitomized the dangers inherent in liberal reforms espoused by Gálvez and Morazán. The acquisition of land and its exploitation by White Creoles and Europeans displaced indigenous communities, rendering the rural poor landless, dependent, and frequently desperate.

The showdown between Carrera and Morazán reached its apex in 1840, when federal troops entered Guatemala and temporarily occupied the capital city in one last attempt by the federal administration to subdue the guerilla counterinsurgency. In March 1840, Carrera's peasant army responded with a devastating retaliatory strike against Morazán's federal army, routing them and driving Morazán into exile. He escaped on a boat to Panama, where he plotted how best to defeat Carrera and restore his federal government.

In 1842, Morazán made one last attempt to crush Carrera's guerilla army and restore the liberal platform he had enacted during his administration. Costa Ricans who sympathized with Carrera's uprising detained Morazán and on September 15, executed him by firing squad in the Costa Rican capital of San José. September 15 thus marked a decisive turning point in modern Central American history. The UPCA's first chief of state died an ignominious death at the hands of is political opponents, a disparate group who had banded together for a common cause.

Morazán's execution signaled the end of the UPCA. As the war subsided and Carrera's influence spread, he systematically dismantled the liberal regime by restoring ecclesiastical privileges, reinstating Spanish judicial procedures, endorsing merchant guilds, and eliminating the head tax.

Carrera's successful confrontations with Gálvez and Morazán won him the support of *mestizos* (mixed Indian and European heritage) and Indians, groups long marginalized by Europeans and liberals. His *mestizo* supporters dominated politics, and his cautious support of indigenous communities stood in stark contrast to the centuries of exploitation they had suffered at the hands of Whites.

Once in power, Carrera's government transformed itself over time into a violent right-wing dictatorship. Like his predecessors, Carrera frequently ruled at gunpoint. Along the way, though, he took a series of steps aimed at reversing liberalism's effects on Guatemala. Poor ladinos and Indians considered the 1837 cholera outbreak God's retribution to liberals, and these same people—the masses—saw as divinely appointed Carrera's efforts to reverse liberal ideals of the 1820s and 1830s.

Carrera reversed many liberal reforms that had undermined the church and central government. His liberal predecessors had expelled various religious orders from Guatemala, and Carrera allowed those orders to return. He restored the church's control over marriage and the registration of births and deaths. Carrera put restrictions on foreign companies whose exploitation of the countryside had disrupted rural life. Throughout his 30-year dictatorship, Carrera left the countryside largely to its own devices, much to the relief of Guatemala's large rural indigenous population.

Over time these steps gained Carrera considerable (though not universal) support in the countryside among Guatemala's rural poor. Ironically, these same steps earned Carrera the support of many of Guatemala's rural wealthy—those who had benefited most directly from the liberal reforms espoused by Gálvez, Morazán and their colleagues in the 1820s and 1830s. Perceiving less danger from foreign land grabbers and reformers, peasant and indigenous communities agitated less during the conservative Carrera dictatorship than they had during the tumultuous liberal era.

The conservative Carrera dictatorship lasted until his death in 1865. Initially he had survived because he placed two loyal strongmen in power, Francisco Ferrera in Honduras and Francisco Malespín in El Salvador. The loyalties of Ferrera and Malespín enabled Carrera to defeat Morazán and consolidate his own power over Guatemala. Then, with the passage of time, his following in Guatemala expanded, and Carrera became a dominant *caudillo*, at once popular with the masses and with sufficient military strength to quell the ambitions of any enemy.

Carrera's death in 1865 created a power vacuum, as conservatives and liberals scrambled to gain control of the government. In 1871, the struggle for power ended when liberals wrested control of the government from conservatives. Beginning with Manuel García Granados and continuing with General Justo Rufino Barrios, liberals launched a number of reforms known in Guatemala history as *La Reforma* (The Reform). This *Reforma* once again took on the church, stripping it of most of its property and removing its control over birth, marriage, and death records.

Emergence of Liberal Dictators

While attacking the church, liberals also resumed their assault on the Guatemalan countryside and its inhabitants. Reformers built roads, installed telegraphs, and opened the land to coffee and banana production. These changes invited increasing numbers of foreigners to exploit Guatemala's wealth of natural resources while displacing ever-increasing numbers of Indians from their villages.

For three decades coffee production accelerated under Barrios's watchful eye. Under the dictatorial guise of "order and progress," Barrios and the liberal dictators who followed him forced thousands of Indians out of their villages and onto new coffee *fincas* (plantations). Guatemala's liberal "reform" administrations made passing reference to the nation's constitution and its democratic processes; in reality, government in Guatemala was dominated by the nation's tiny White elite at the expense of its large, majority indigenous population. In practice, throughout the liberal era most Guatemalans experienced the persistent loss of their most basic rights and freedoms while losing their ability to provide for themselves.

After Barrios's death in 1885, a series of liberal dictators contin-ued enacting liberal reforms. Perhaps most vicious of all was Manuel Estrada Cabrera, who governed from 1898 until he was removed form the presidency in 1920 when Guatemala's Congress declared him insane. Estrada Cabrera was ruthless in his pursuit of liberal secularization, justifying his excesses as necessity: "The glo-rious priesthood of the Law in the majestic temple of Justice on the unyielding rock of the Truth."

Like Central America's other liberal dictators, Estrada Cabrera argued in favor of progress and development, and he promoted the secularization of education as a necessary measure to prolong Guatemala's economic advances. His pro-education rhetoric per-haps placated some corners of Guatemalan society, but when Estrada Cabrera left office, 86 percent of all Guatemalans remained illiterate. Meanwhile, Guatemala's natural resources became increasingly con-centrated due, in part, to his reforms. When World War I began, Germans grew half of all coffee produced in Guatemala, and by the mid-1920s, only 7.3 percent of the people owned land. Amazingly, liberal reforms had created a huge class of landless peasants who had to migrate to large coffee *fincas* (plantations) in order to subsist. These realities severely alienated the vast majority of Guatemala's population, as demonstrated by the fact that Guatemalans made several unsuccessful attempts on Estrada Cabrera's life. In the end, however, he controlled the military and was therefore able to survive even ardent opposition to his administration.

Things did not improve after Estrada Cabrera's ouster in 1920. After a decade of chaos in the 1920s, Jorge Ubico assumed the presidency and began yet another violent dictatorship. He reorga-nized the nation's secret police and used it to terrorize his political opponents, which included much of Guatemala's predominantly indigenous citizenry. Ubico accelerated road construction in the interior, promoted massive foreign investment by offering large concessions to foreign financiers, decimated workers' organizations, and removed the autonomy of universities he believed promoted political dissent (most famously the University of San Carlos). He enacted *Ley de Vialidad* (Public Roadways Law), requiring two weeks per year of obligatory public service, a responsibility that could also be met by a specified cash payment. Those who had the financial wherewithal to make this payment avoided public ser-vice; those who could not afford the payment worked two weeks each year on public works projects.

In addition to enacting the Public Roadways Law, Ubico further alienated Guatemala's working poor when he enacted a repressive vagrancy law that required all persons who owned less than a stipulated amount of land to carry cards with them indicating that they had worked at least 150 days per year on one of the nation's large plantations. As barely 7 percent of Guatemalans owned land, this meant that a huge majority of the population would be bound by vagrancy and roadway laws. Anyone who could not produce this card on demand went to jail or directly to a public works project.

Having assumed the presidency during the Great Depression, Ubico was particularly violent in his efforts to contain popular unrest. With an economy based largely on coffee, Guatemala was devastated when world coffee prices dropped severely in the mid-1930s. World War II further exacerbated the problem by cutting off the flow of goods to and from Europe, and considered collectively the Depression and the war resulted in widespread unemployment, wage reductions, and business failures for many small merchants and landowners. As these crises unfolded and the outlook for working Guatemalans became increasingly bleak, government repression increased proportionately. As historian Benjamin Keen has pointed out, in 1933, the government executed more than 100 labor leaders and other political dissidents, not to mention hundreds of workers and activists who did not occupy prominent positions.

Confronted with an increasingly ruthless dictator, Guatemalans took matters into their own hands in June 1944. That month, widespread strikes and anti-Ubico demonstrations forced the dictator to resign. In the short term, this victory for anti-Ubico forces accentuated the strength of the nation's poor when they acted in unison. This turn of events convinced Guatemala's wealthy that communism threatened their way of life. For 10 years two popularly elected presidents governed Guatemala after Ubico's resignation, only to be ousted once again by the nation's rich and powerful, as well as their foreign benefactor, the U.S. Central Intelligence Agency. Further, the 1954 overthrow of an elected president would begin decades of bloody civil war wherein many tens of thousands would die at the hands of military officers doing the government's bidding.

A Ten-Year Experiment with Democracy

In December 1944, Guatemalans elected Juan José Arévalo President of the Republic. Arévalo, a professor who had been in exile for many years, favored the establishment of democracy while focusing on improving social issues. Arévalo abolished the hated vagrancy law and launched a series of reforms aimed at making hospitals and schools more widely accessible to Guatemalans of all backgrounds. In 1947, his administration promoted the establishment of a labor code that provided collective bargaining rights for workers, who could join the union of their choice. Tellingly, worker's wages rose nearly 80 percent during Arévalo's administration, and his progressive labor reform enabled agricultural workers to challenge their employers, including the United Fruit Company (UFCO). Urban labor benefited most from these measures, but Arévalo made only mild progress in the countryside. It would be up to his successor to extend these reforms to the countryside.

Arévalo's reforms made numerous enemies inside and outside Guatemala. He survived 25 assassination attempts, and much of the officer corps objected strenuously to the restlessness his reforms caused both in the cities and in the countryside. Moreover, UFCO distrusted his pro-labor attitude and feared where such ideas might lead. UFCO owned 550,000 acres of land in Guatemala, and barely 15 percent was being used. The remainder lay fallow; that is, it went totally unused from one year to the next. UFCO officials feared any discussion of workers' rights or land reform because they stood to lose a tremendous amount of money and interests.

HONDURAS

Much of Honduras's modern history has been defined by its supporting roles in regional conflicts. It has the misfortune of sharing borders with Guatemala, El Salvador, and Nicaragua—three nations wrought with civil strife and political violence throughout much of the national period.

In the 1820s and 1830s, native son Francisco Morazán led a liberal movement that brought him into conflict with the region's conservatives, including the church. More recently Honduras has been surrounded by nations whose civil wars spilled over into their homelands, forcing Hondurans to take sides in conflicts that would have no clear winners. This frequently troubled history has left Honduras struggling to deal with an economy in tatters, highly dependent on the United States, and a restive military that has tended to intervene and topple governments when threatened. The last several decades' dialectic between Honduras's military and its civil authorities suggests that the conservative-liberal struggle first championed by Morazán continues today to define political and economic life in Honduras.

Early Liberalism

Considered by many to be the "spiritual father of liberalism" in Central America, Francisco Morazán first gained fame when, in 1829, he led an overmatched ragtag liberal army who defeated an entrenched conservative army in several battles. As a result, Morazán became President of the United Provinces of Central America in 1830. Once in office, he enacted a series of reforms aimed at liberalizing education, the church, the judicial system, and land distribution. He spent much of the next decade invading regions where recalcitrant conservatives resisted the tide of change.

In 1837, conservative Rafael Carrera's success in the War of the Mountain marked a turning point for Morazán. Carrera had the support of wealthy landowners and the church, who provided him support and contact with the countryside that proved particularly valuable. Ultimately, Carrera's forces drove Morazán into exile in 1840. Two years later, Morazán returned from exile, intent on trying once more to unify all of Central America into a liberal state. During this return, he was shot and killed by one of his own troops on September 15, 1842.

One of the rare moments when Hondurans came together with other Central Americans occurred in the 1850s, when American William Walker invaded Nicaragua and declared himself president. Eventually, all the Central American states sided with Nicaraguans in the desire to oust Walker. In 1857, he surrendered to the U.S. navy, only to renew his efforts to conquer and govern all of Central America. This second escapade ended when Walker was captured by the British navy, which turned him over to Honduras. On September 12, 1860, Honduras executed Walker by firing squad.

Over the course of the next several decades, the liberal-conservative conflict ebbed and flowed in Honduras. In 1876, Marco Aurelio Soto became president of Honduras. Soto, a protégé of Barrios in Guatemala, attempted to proceed with liberal reforms in Honduras like those occurring elsewhere in the region. In an effort to spur coffee exports, Soto tried to construct an interoceanic railroad connecting the Gulf of Cortés in the Gulf of Honduras with the Gulf of Fonseca on the Pacific Coast. A combination of political corruption and runaway costs doomed the project, which failed miserably. The failure of the railway system, in turn, doomed Soto's plan to increase coffee exports; Honduras's rugged terrain made rapid development impossible.

In the mid-1890s, President Policarpo Bonilla continued Soto's program of liberal reforms, and, with the firm support of Nicaraguan liberals, accomplished much in the realm of institutional reforms. In the end, however, a number of insurmountable difficulties prevented significant reform that would result in economic growth and diversification. The nation's prohibitive terrain and lack of an effective means of transportation kept Honduras badly fragmented along regional lines, and an extremely tenuous communications system prevented all but the most rudimentary forms of interregional communications. As Costa Rican scholar Hector Pérez-Brignoli points out, the combination of these hardships gave neighboring states considerable influence in Honduran matters. The disproportionate pull wielded by neighboring states contributed powerfully to Honduras's instability.

Carías and Militarism

Into this fray stepped the "velvet-gloved" military dictator, Tiburcio Carías Andino. Carías became president in 1932, and although he was a military contemporary of Estrada Cabrera and Ubico, Carías proved less ruthless. His "benevolence" resulted largely from his relationship with the United Fruit Company. In 1929, a divisive and prolonged competition between UFCO and the Cuyamel Fruit Company ended when the two merged, meaning that Honduras's politicians would pander to one company and one group of employees. When Carías became president in 1932, he dealt gently with UFCO and promoted economic expansion that hinged largely on UFCO's success; the company and the dictator had common interests that made them mutually dependent.

As president, Carías took a series of steps to ensure that he could protect the interests of foreign companies doing business in Honduras, thus gaining support for his dictatorship from the United States and from wealthy Hondurans, two groups that found comfort in Carías's willingness to suppress Communist activity in Honduras. In 1934, for example, Carías took the extraordinary step of establishing a military aviation school, and he appointed a U.S. army colonel as commandant of the new school. In 1935, he outlawed the Communist Party of Honduras, and during this same period, he gained the support and unwavering gratitude of the foreign banana companies when he used the military to crush strikes and unrest among the nation's farm workers.

With the support and popularity these steps gave him among the investment communities and the foreign fruit companies, Carías now moved to extend his tenure as president. He convened a constitutional assembly to amend Honduras's constitution and make it legal for him to remain in office. The plan worked, and he remained in office until 1949.

Of particular significance during Carías's dictatorship is the cordial relationship he forged with the other military dictators of Central America: Generals Jorge Ubico in Guatemala, Maximiliano Hernández Martínez in El Salvador, and Anastasio Somoza García in Nicaragua. Carías was particularly close to Ubico, who helped him reorganize his secret police and also captured and shot the leader of a Honduran uprising who had crossed into Guatemalan territory in an attempt to flee reprisals from the Carías administration.

NICARAGUA

Like other nations in nineteenth-century Central America, Nicaragua's economy was dominated by coffee. The nation's coffee exports increased rapidly between 1850 and 1870, and by 1890 it was responsible for the majority of the nation's export earnings. Cattle and bananas also generated significant income, but coffee was "king" in the export sector.

The intersection of money and politics in early twentieth-century Nicaragua came to a head during the tumultuous presidency of General José Santos Zelaya (1893–1909). A ruthless military dictator, Zelaya promoted a variety of liberal initiatives. He enacted anticlerical initiatives, opened the nation to foreign investment, and increased exports of bananas and coffee. As president, he oversaw the construction of an excellent new export infrastructure—new roads, new rail lines, and new sea ports. Moreover, despite being anti-American, Zelaya invited U.S. financiers to participate fully in the liberalization of the Nicaraguan economy. By the early twentieth century, U.S. financiers controlled Nicaragua's banana, coffee, gold, and lumber industries.

As would be the case elsewhere in Central America, increased U.S. interests in Nicaragua resulted in military invasions when the United States believed their newly acquired interests were at risk. When Zelaya invited the Japanese and Germans to compete with the United States for a canal route across Nicaragua, he crossed the proverbial "line in the sand." The United States did not take lightly a nation that used its resources to blackmail the U.S. government, and officials in Washington decided to act. In 1909, 400 U.S. marines landed in Nicaragua and helped overthrow the Zelaya dictatorship. The permanent U.S. military occupation of Nicaragua lasted from 1909 to 1933, when U.S. officials armed and trained a Nicaraguan *Guardia Nacional* (National Guard) to step in and defend U.S. concerns once Washington withdrew its troops.

When U.S. military forces left Nicaragua for the last time in 1933, they left a hand-picked commander of the new National Guard that would govern Nicaragua in the absence of Yanqui troops. This new commander, Anastasio Somoza García, soon proved himself a tyrannical military dictator who governed Nicaragua with an iron fist. First indications of Somoza's ruthlessness occurred on February 21, 1934, after Augusto César Sandino attended a special dinner with Nicaragua's elected president, Juan B. Sacasa. Sandino had carried on a years-long struggle against occupying American forces and, when the last of the Americans had withdrawn, Sacasa invited Sandino to the presidential palace in Managua to establish a cordial working relationship. Sacasa had personally guaranteed Sandino's safety, and yet as the nationalist patriot left the palace, National Guard Commander Somoza arrested Sandino. The Guard then took Sandino to the airfield and executed him.

The Somoza Dynasty

After the murder of Sandino, Somoza continued to openly defy President Sacasa. In 1936, Somoza ran for president, taking care to incorporate control of the National Guard into his duties as president-elect. From his election in 1936 to his assassination in 1956, Somoza used the presidency to enrich himself and his family while brutally suppressing any economic or political dissidence. A few brief years into his presidency, Somoza had consolidated control of Nicaragua's political system, economy, and military. Somoza was an amazingly selfish, brutal dictator, and his control of his nation's resources exceeded that of any of his dictatorial peers in Central America. Certainly Guatemala's Ubico never approached this level of domination, and Somoza probably had more thorough control of his country than the oligarchy/military tandem in El Salvador.

The outbreak of World War II helped galvanize Somoza's control. The dictator supported the Allies's war efforts from the beginning of the war, and in return Nicaragua received large quantities of support from the United States. Washington relaxed trade restrictions on Latin America just as Europe's markets mobilized for war, and Nicaraguan exports to the United States soared, particularly cotton, gold, and timber. Beginning in 1942, the Somoza dictatorship also received $872,841.73 in Lend-Lease military assistance, which further professionalized the nation's armed forces. Although this aid was meager when compared to the Lend-Lease distributed in Europe, the small number of armored vehicles and weapons Nicaragua received dramatically strengthened Somoza's domestic iron fist.

CONCLUSIONS

As the new nations of El Salvador, Guatemala, Honduras, and Nicaragua took shape after independence, the seeds were sewn for violent military dictatorships midway through the twentieth century. The ongoing clash between liberals and conservatives established battle lines that would divide these nations through much of the their modern history. Throughout the late nineteenth and twentieth centuries, liberals throughout all of Central America favored free trade, modernization of the economy, incentives to attract foreign investment, and close control of the church. Conversely, conservatives favored restoration of the Catholic church to a position of preeminence, trade controlled more closely by the central government, and preservation of local customs and traditions instead of Westernization.

These fundamental differences factored heavily into the later cold war era. Liberals who favored economic expansion and modernity received overwhelming support from the United States, which saw the struggle in Central America as a clash between capitalism and communism—good versus evil. Those conservative factions that favored more traditional values—the centrality of the church in Central American culture, concern for the poor, distrust of rapid foreign expansion on their soil—came to be known in the United

States (and, consequently, among its allies in Central America) as Communist sympathizers. The most notable example is Archbishop Romero, who was murdered in 1980 by a military death squad who accused him of being a Communist sympathizer.

As the twentieth century began, rapid industrialization and World War I made the United States an economic powerhouse to be reckoned with. U.S. financial interests in Central America increased rapidly after the war, and Central American politicians soon found it helpful to protect U.S. interests in their respective nations. In the 1930s, the dictators identified in this chapter grew powerful and wealthy by defending U.S. interests in their countries, and U.S. politicians and businessmen became increasingly brazen in their support of violent military dictators in the name of fighting communism. The problem with this strategy, of course, is that poor people, priests, students, and those who opposed a large foreign presence in their country were not necessarily Communists. Such matters would be an issue when the United States became more fully engaged in Central America during the early decades of the twentieth century.

NOTE

1. A death squad generally consist of off-duty soldiers or police who are hired by landowners, industrialists, or politicians to "disappear" a political enemy. In the 1970s and 1980s, death squads killed tens of thousands of Central Americans. The United States would officially back much of this activity.

4

Panama: From Colombian Province to Occupied State

As had been the case in the pre-historic and colonial eras, Panama followed its own path to independence, autonomy, and development during the nineteenth and twentieth centuries. The size of Panama's coffee crop and its export economy generally pales in comparison to other Central American countries. Conversely, for better or worse its link to the developing world economy in the nineteenth and twentieth centuries exceeded that of any other country because of its strategic location; its exportable raw material was its location. Cochineal, indigo, and even coffee economies suffered occasionally at the hands of world demand, but passage from sea to sea via the shortest route never fell out of season. As long as politicians and merchants needed to get from one ocean to the other as quickly and safely as possible, a market would always exist for Panama's greatest raw material.

On November 28, 1821, 31 of Panama's leading landowners and merchants convened to declare their independence from Spain. Ill-equipped to defend themselves from Spanish reprisals, these leading citizens then annexed the isthmus to Simón Bolívar's *Gran Colombia*, a newly established entity with which Panama's elite had much in common. Wealthy merchants in Panama City and

Bogotá shared a common interest in secure trade across Panama, and this alliance met these concerns; Panama would generate for Colombia a large amount of revenue as the principal point of transshipment between the oceans. Meanwhile, residents of Panama City and Portobelo would service those transshipments, making a fortune in their monopoly of the shipping industry.

Merchants in Panama quickly realized that their alliance with Bogotá left them vulnerable to exploitation, as they watched the large portion of money earned in Panama being sent to merchants and officials in Bogotá. Just as Guatemalans had quickly wearied of their subordinate relationship with Mexico, Panamanian merchants soon came to resent being subordinate to officials and banks in distant Bogotá.

A POPULAR CONSCIENCE

Early relations between Panama City and Bogotá proved cumbersome and divisive. Officials in Bogotá had allowed wealthy merchants in Panama to trade freely with friendly nations, but this attempt by Bogotá overlooked the race and class compositions of Colombia's northern countryside. Much of Colombia's restive Caribbean coast was Black, as was urban Panama. Bogotá's generosity with Panama's tiny merchant elite excluded the region's large population of Black urban poor. These attempts by Colombian officials at placating Panama's small white merchant population seriously alienated Blacks living in Gran Colombia's northern reaches, including Panama. These race problems were further exacerbated when Bolívar and his appointees based suffrage on property requirements (land ownership), thus disenfranchising most of Panama's Black population, which formed a part of Colombia's Black liberals, those Blacks who favored racial equality, states' rights, and laissez-faire economics. Thus, early in Panama's history, a popular class conscience emerged, with Panama's large Black population recoiling against its subservience to Whites.

In 1830, the first tangible evidence of this popular class conscience surfaced when a mulatto, José Domingo Espinar, began a separatist movement among the urban poor in Panama City. Espinar, formerly Simón Bolívar's personal secretary, used his political experience to fashion Panama City's urban masses into a formidable, well-organized group with common goals. Espinar's separatist movement actually achieved control of Panama City for several months in 1830, while Colombian officials and White Panamanians reeled, declaring Panama's independence from Colombia September 26 of that year.

Whites in Panama feared a repeat of the slave uprising that had occurred in Haiti at the turn of the century, and they took steps to regain control of the situation. Conservative Governor José de Obaldía went as far as accusing Espinar of organizing a "caste war" against Panama's White population. Espinar's response proved more enduring than his separatist movement, which was soon crushed. Espinar responded that Governor Obaldía "must have recently undergone a profound organic alteration of the brain."

Espinar's uprising underscores a peculiarity of Panama's political situation at the time. Elsewhere in Spanish America, ownership of the means of production afforded the governing elite a mechanism of control when things got out of hand. When threatened, cochineal barons in Guatemala (for example) could use their control of peasant livelihoods as a means of coercion. Particularly through the reign of Carrera, landowners could use their control of land as a negotiating mechanism to achieve their bargaining objectives. Elites in Panama had no such mechanism of leverage. When threatened by Espinar, Panama's ruling elite had to choose between two unpalatable options: be governed by a separatist movement composed largely of angry Black poor, or ask Colombian troops to intervene and save them. Panama's wealthy chose to ask Colombian troops for help, and, in late 1831, Colombian Colonel Juan Eligio Alzuru ended Espinar's rebellion and restored Colombian control.

For the first time in Panama's history, its governing elite had asked foreign troops to intervene in their behalf. Given their unique predicament—they did not own the means of local livelihood—Panama City's elite used the only mechanism of leverage at their disposal: foreign military intervention. This scene would repeat itself more than two dozen times over the next two centuries, culminating with a massive invasion by American military forces in December 1989 that left thousands dead and homeless.

"FEDERALISM"

A second problem emerged shortly after independence from Spain that similarly strained Panama's ties to Bogotá. By the mid-nineteenth century, much of Panama's wealthy worked in its transportation industry, providing warehousing needs to merchants transshipping goods across the Isthmus. Many of these same wealthy owned urban properties that they rented to people crossing the Isthmus, helping them along the way. Over time, these urban wealthy increasingly resented the taxes and tariffs they were required to send to Bogotá. These nationalist activists agitated increasingly against Colombian (and foreign) intervention.

In the mid-1850s, one of the most visible of these middle-class activists, Justo Arosemena, became the most vocal advocate for Panama's independence from Colombia. Arosemena believed that Panama would become "an emporium of world commerce," and he opposed quite vocally Colombia's political and economic jurisdiction on the Isthmus. He contended (correctly) that Bogotá siphoned off huge sums of money in the form of taxes that ought to have remained in Panama. He argued for an autonomous Panamanian government that could administer the Isthmus's economic and legal affairs while keeping profits from Panama's transportation industry in Panama.

In 1855, the United States finished constructing the Panama Railroad. The next year, Arosemena argued against "Yankee intervention," just as he had clamored against Colombian intervention. For the first time, anti-Americanism became political currency on the Isthmus, a process accelerated and reaffirmed by Washington's repeated military invasions of Panama during the next 150 years.

A FALSE SENSE OF PROSPERITY

Under the Bourbon reforms of the eighteenth century, Spain had increased the number of ports where merchants could legally trade with Spanish America. This removed Panama's monopoly on trade between the Andes and Europe, and the amount of commerce crossing the Isthmus declined precipitously. With little compelling them to remain in Panama City, much of the Isthmus's tiny elite moved to their ranches deep in Panama's interior, where they maintained a small –but flourishing cattle industry.[1]

Events in the first decades of the nineteenth century reversed the out-migration triggered by Bourbon policies. The discovery of gold along the California coast helped spur the completion of the Panama Railroad, which, when completed in 1855, facilitated safe, rapid transit for Forty-Niners rushing to stake their claims. The combination of the gold rush and the completed railway drew increasing numbers of wealthy Hispanics back to the city, where they again invested heavily in the transit industry. Wealthy Panamanians assumed second-tier administrative posts with the railroad while investing heavily in rental properties and related service-sector businesses such as warehouses.

The initial economic flurry triggered by the forty-niners sparked what one Panamanian scholar has called, "a false sense of prosperity." Rental prices spiked as demand soared, causing a housing frenzy among the urban elite who rushed to capitalize on large waves of foreigners crossing Panama en route between the coasts of North America.

The boom triggered by the gold rush profoundly affected life in Panama. Thousands of Black West Indians had gone to Panama to help build the railroad, and, on its completion, many lacked the resources necessary to return to their homelands, remaining instead in Panama. This large population of unemployed railroad laborers joined many hundreds of oarsmen and mule train drivers put permanently out of work by the completion of the railroad.

Panama's wealthy fared little better. For several years after the completion of the railroad, waves of prospectors continued to flood across Panama. As the gold rush tapered off, however, so, too, did the demand for Panama's expanded service-sector economy. British and American financiers who had invested in the railroad and its related industries continued to make money once prospector traffic stopped. Despite the cessation of the gold frenzy, the railroad continued to offer travelers a faster, safer, easier journey from coast to coast. Conversely, Panamanian capital had been invested almost entirely in the housing and service industries, which effectively dried up once California's gold veins ceased producing windfall fortunes. As had been the case when the Bourbon reforms had ended Panama's monopoly on commerce between Europe and the Andes, Panama's economic elite once again found themselves struggling to survive yet another change in world commerce.

Circumstances surrounding the completion of the railroad and the end of the gold rush frayed race and class relations on the Isthmus. The railroad also strained Panama City's relations with Bogotá. Railroad officials paid Colombia $250,000 per year for land and necessary rights to operate the railroad, but Bogotá sent only $25,000 of that money back to Panama. Panama's albatross was Colombia's cash cow.

THE LIMITS OF LIBERALISM

The 1850s and 1860s proved a heady time for Colombia. Coffee prices were high, as were returns on Colombia's other cash crops—indigo, tobacco, and rubber. As had been the case in Guatemala during the Carrera regime, a strong economy placated all concerned, including both wealthy investors and peasant laborers. Circumstances during economic good times required minimal oversight, and to this end liberals in Bogotá enacted a liberal constitution that significantly reduced Colombia's military and administrative presence throughout the countryside, including in Panama.

During times of economic windfall, this liberalization made sense. The government's reduced presence improved relations with its rural provinces, where more jobs and higher wages accomplished what required rifles and soldiers during times of economic duress. By pushing states' rights so emphatically, though, Bogotá significantly reduced its ability to govern the hinterlands, particularly the northern coastal regions of Bolívar, Magdalena, and Panama. Circumstances would underscore the limits of liberalism two decades later, when world markets constricted and prices fell sharply.

THE *COMPAGNIE UNIVERSELLE DU CANAL INTEROCÉANIQUE* (THE UNIVERSAL COMPANY OF THE INTEROCEANIC CANAL)

For wealthy Panamanians in the 1870s, Frenchman Ferdinand De Lesseps seemed an act of providence. De Lesseps began digging the Suez Canal in 1857 despite widespread derision for what many considered a silly idea. Yet, in 1869, De Lesseps's seemingly impossible dream came true when the Suez Canal opened for business. For several years afterwards, De Lesseps studied world commerce and concluded that he needed to build a second great waterway, this one through Panama. In 1879, De Lesseps pitched his proposal at an international conference in Paris. The majority of conference participants embraced the concept of a Panama Canal and named De Lesseps leader of the new *Compagnie Universelle du Canal Interocéanique.*

De Lesseps had never been to Panama and he was not an engineer. When the Paris conference began, a French engineer named

Godin de Lépinay called De Lesseps's plan for a sea-level canal across Panama suicidal, and instead proposed a canal-and-locks system that closely reflected the American plan that succeeded a few decades later.[2] De Lesseps's plan for a sea-level canal carried the day, though, and the *Compagnie* began planning how best to accomplish this monumental task.

Panama's wealthy hoped that the French canal project would breathe new life into their economy, and they were not disappointed. The influx of thousands of French citizens during the project (1881–1889) temporarily resuscitated Panama's moribund economy. Two things happened in the 1880s, though, that upset this relative sense of equilibrium. First, the French were failing in their attempt to master Panama's difficult terrain. Second, economic realities elsewhere in Colombia had turned sour in the mid-1880s, and conservatives were now moving to control both the economic difficulties Colombia faced and the unrest caused by those difficulties.

RAFAEL NÚÑEZ AND COLOMBIA'S *REGENERACIÓN*

In the late 1870s and early 1880s, sharp declines in world demand for coffee, indigo, rubber, and tobacco dramatically reversed the giddy economic trends of the 1860s. Among Colombia's laborers, these changes meant fewer jobs and lower wages. Unemployment rose, dissatisfaction increased, and strikes once again became prominent as workers' nerves and patience became frayed. Yet, the 1863 constitution had severely limited Bogotá's ability to quell the violence and restore order. Into this set of circumstances stepped Rafael Núñez, one of the more colorful politicians anywhere in the Americas.

Rafael Núñez began his political career as a radical liberal who supported the 1863 constitution and supported states' rights. Then, for more than a decade he served as a Colombian diplomat in Europe, where he devoted considerable time to studying European political and economic thought. When he returned to Colombia in 1875, Núñez became convinced that Colombia needed a restoration of conservative values. As he witnessed the effects of market stagnation on Colombia's economy and stability, he became convinced that the only way to promote "progress and order" was to reinstitute the conservative, centralized state that had dominated Colombia during the first decades of independence. Núñez believed a strong military and an equally strong federal police force to be the only means of accomplishing this objective.

In 1880, he ascended to the presidency of the Colombia and began to implement sweeping reforms aimed at restoring the national government's prestige and ability to govern. Elected again in 1884, Núñez launched *La Regeneración,* (regeneration, restoration) a series of sweeping conservative steps aimed at undoing the *Reforma* of the 1860s. Among other things, Núñez's *Regeneración*:

- Announced the 1863 constitution had "ceased to exist"
- Proposed and enacted a new constitution in 1886, which replaced state governors with new state governors appointed by the president
- Extended presidential terms to six years
- Based suffrage on literacy and property requirements
- Made Catholicism Colombia's official religion
- Restored several clergy privileges removed by liberals, including mandating that education at all levels in Colombia be made to conform with Catholic doctrine

This last point had significant influence among Colombians. At a time when Jeremy Bentham and other liberal authors promoted secular education and roundly rejected creationism, Núñez's decision to give the church control of education granted priests veto power over textbooks that they deemed objectionable and doctrinally false. *La Regeneración* ensured that secularism would not form part of education at any level in Colombia.

Núñez ruled Colombia in this fashion until his death in 1894. His "progressive dictatorship" had many similarities to Guatemala's own *Reforma* and the strident policies of Barrios. His policies frequently favored the rich at the expense of the poor, and the *La Regeneración* alienated millions of Colombian peasants.

THOUSAND DAYS' WAR AND PANAMA'S INDEPENDENCE

For these and other reasons, *La Regeneración* forms an integral part of Panamanian history. Just as the French canal effort was taking off and Panama's urban elites once again began seeing returns on their urban real estate investments, Colombia returned to a heavy-handed means of administering Panama. Núñez alienated Panama's elite when he increased taxes, implemented forced loans to the government, and returned to the practice of placing customs houses in Panama, a practice that had been outlawed in March 1835. He disenfranchised Panama's poor by basing suffrage on literacy and property qualifications, thus ending universal male suffrage on the Isthmus.

While the French project moved forward, most Panamanians remained placated. The poor had jobs and the rich had money to pay the elevated taxes demanded by Bogotá. The benefits they received from the French outweighed resentment of *bogotano* intervention. The failure of the De Lesseps project, however, had the same effect on Panamanians as declining coffee prices had on residents elsewhere in Central America.

The elite began considering their options in the face of Núñez's heavy-handedness, and the protests of the urban poor reached a crescendo in the mid-1880s. Living conditions among Panama City's working poor were deplorable long before the *Regeneración* began, and Núñez's tax reforms and vagrancy laws pushed life in Panama City's urban poor to the crisis stage.

Under these conditions, in early 1885, two mulatto leaders, Rafael Aizpuru and Pedro Prestán, took matters into their own hands. Apparently functioning independently of one another, Aizpuru and Prestán took control of Panama City and Colón with the support of the working-class populations of both cities.[3] They controlled the two cities for several months, but after a now-established pattern of response, Panama's elite requested armed assistance from Colombia and the United States. Colombian troops, with support from 1,200 U.S. troops, fought their way into the two cities and ended the uprising. In August Prestán was publicly hanged in an ad hoc gallows in Colón, signaling a violent end to yet another uprising among Panama's large urban working class.

By 1890, conditions in Panama had degenerated dangerously. In 1885, the urban poor had seen their protests violently subdued, and then in 1889 the French canal project collapsed, once again stranding tens of thousands of unemployed foreign Black workers. Also, Panama's merchant class and economic elite found their hopes once again dashed and their fortunes jeopardized by a failed foreign economic initiative on the Isthmus.

Independence

Núñez's *Regeneración* helped only a small portion of Colombia's population: political and financial elites, wealthy merchants, and foreigners wishing to do business in Colombia. His financial policies profoundly affected life for the nation's poor, however, and when they began clamoring for change, he reverted to violence. Núñez made the National Police a permanent institution and enacted laws that gave the military a monopoly on the use of force in Colombia. His 1886 constitution reserved for the central government the exclusive right to bear arms and ammunition. Any resistance to his policies would be thwarted violently, and he ensured that any battle with his troops would not be a fair fight.

Under these circumstances, peasants throughout rural Colombia began resisting these reforms. Protests erupted throughout the countryside, including Panama. After Núñez's death in 1894, the clash continued between conservatives and liberals, culminating in 1899 with the outbreak of a bloody three-year civil war known as the *Guerra de los Mil Días* (The Thousand-Days' War, 1899–1902). This war cost Colombia 100,000 lives and vast economic destruction.

At the height of the Thousand-Days' War, Panamanian nationalists led by Belisario Porras took up arms in an attempt to permanently expel Colombian troops from Panama. From July 1900–October 1902, these nationalists fought tenaciously to drive Colombians from Panama. In October 1902 Porras's insurgent forces abandoned their efforts and surrendered, effectively ending the conflict.

While this peace accord effectively ended the pitched battles in and around the capital city, many of Panama's rural poor objected to Porras's decision to capitulate and continued fighting. Most notable among these rural rebels was Victoriano Lorenzo, a Guaymí Indian from Coclé in north-central Panama. Lorenzo refused to surrender his weapons when the peace accord was signed, and he continued to lead an effective guerilla insurgency against Colombian soldiers and against former comrades who had capitulated in a peace treaty.

Lorenzo's continued resistance epitomized the division between poor Panamanians in rural areas and urban Panamanians who stood to gain from foreign commerce transiting the Isthmus. Porras and his urban middle-class followers had fought for control of Panama's commercial sector; Lorenzo and his fellow guerilla fighters had fought for Panama's independence and for the expulsion of foreigners from the Isthmus—including foreigners who had gone to Panama to seek their fortunes.

In a tragic turn of events, an armed group consisting of Colombian troops and Panamanian nationalists arrested Lorenzo and took him to Panama City, where they charged him with inciting insurgency and threatening the stability of the government. On May 15, 1903, Lorenzo was executed by hanging. Murdered by a group that included many Panamanians, Lorenzo's death became a rallying point for all Panamanians opposed to foreign encroachment and elite manipulation. Understandably, he became the martyred hero of the nationalist crusade.

In December 1901, the United States and Great Britain had signed the Hay-Pauncefote Treaty, an agreement wherein Great Britain ceded to Washington the right to build and control a canal across Central America. In the wake of the Spanish-American War, President Theodore Roosevelt believed a canal across Central America to be critical to future American security. In June 1902, the Spooner Bill mandated that Panama be the site of the unfolding American canal project. In the Hay-Herrán Treaty of January 1903, Colombia consented to give Washington a 100-year lease to build and operate a canal across Panama, and plans for the American canal project seemed to be approaching fruition. The Colombian legislature never ratified the Hay-Herrán agreement, however, and by mid-1903, Bogotá's opposition to the accord became clear. In July 1903, a revolutionary junta composed of prominent Panamanians began lobbying for American intervention. This group of wealthy Panamanians, headed by Dr. Manuel Amador Guerrero, wanted the United States to complete the canal project left behind by the French, and by this point Washington clearly wanted to undertake the project, so neither side needed much cajoling. Theodore Roosevelt was infuriated by Colombia's foot-dragging and quickly embraced the idea proposed by Guerrero and his supporters.

Beginning in October 1903, the Panamanian revolutionary junta began agitating against Colombian officials in Panama. Then, with the support of the United States, the junta declared Panama's independence from Colombia on November 3, 1903. Colombia's ability to defend its sovereign interests in Panama were badly hampered by the presence of the American battleship, *U.S.S. Nashville*. In a stunning display of gunboat diplomacy, U.S. forces prevented Colombian troops from landing. In the absence of Colombian troops to thwart the uprising, the insurgency succeeded with amazing rapidity and with a minimum of bloodshed: the revolt was over in one day, with one death and minimal destruction.

Having gained their independence, insurgent leaders moved quickly to bolster their new nation. In circumstances eerily similar to Panama's independence from Spain in 1821, Guerrero and his compatriots looked to Washington to replace Colombia as the patron of Panamanian independence. The revolutionary junta appointed Frenchman Philippe Bunau-Varilla as their diplomatic representative to Washington. Bunau-Varilla, who had invested heavily in the French canal project, stood to recover a significant amount of money if the United States moved ahead with its plans for a canal in Panama. In the months before Panama's independence, Bunau-Varilla had helped arrange financial support for the insurgents. In return for this support, the junta appointed him their diplomatic representative to Washington and instructed him not to sign any agreements until Guerrero and his entourage arrived days later.

Bunau-Varilla's appointment is a defining crucible in modern Panamanian history. Instead of honoring his appointment, the Frenchman disregarded his diplomatic charge and signed a treaty with Secretary of State John Hay that completely disregarded Panamanian interests. In exchange for the $10 million sale of the French project to the Americans, Bunau-Varilla agreed to a canal treaty with the United States that granted Washington a 10-mile wide strip of land between Panama City and Colón, Panama's premier commercial real estate. Worse still, he granted the U.S. government sovereign control of this prime piece of real estate "in perpetuity"—forever.

When Amador arrived at the Washington train station, he was greeted by Bunau-Varilla, who informed him of the agreement. Devastated, Amador slapped the Frenchman on the cheek with a glove. The deed was done, however, and Panamanians could do nothing to reverse the agreement.

Completed on November 18, 1903, the Hay-Bunau-Varilla Treaty formed the nucleus of anti-Americanism in Panama and throughout much of Latin America for the duration of the twentieth century. Two facets of this accord angered (understandably) generations of Panamanians. First, Bunau-Varilla's treasonous act ensured that no Panamanian could be present at the signing to object to the conditions of the agreement. Second, the United States exploited the reviled treaty while completely disregarding the sovereign concerns of the new republic.

Under these conditions, Panama began the twentieth century as it had the nineteenth, as well as every century since the Europeans arrived: beholden to a foreign country that maintained a large military presence on the Isthmus. Since the early sixteenth century, Panama had been occupied by foreigners intent on exploiting Panama and quite willing to use violence if Panamanians objected too strenuously.

OCCUPATION "IN PERPETUITY"

The United States began constructing the Panama Canal in 1904, and successfully completed it in 1914 as war erupted in Europe. Now open to world commerce, the canal cut 8,000 nautical miles off the trip between the east and west coasts of the United States. Traffic began slowly, but over time a large percentage of the world's commerce took advantage of the shortcut. Tactically, the canal enabled U.S. war planners to move ships and armaments between oceans with a minimum of time and expense. For American politicians, the strategic value of the canal made Panama one of the most important spots on the globe for the defense of the United States. Throughout World War II, the U.S. military and the State Department considered Panama and Hawaii the two most strategically significant spots in the world outside the United States. This strategically sensitive ranking ensured that money and jobs would remain in Panama "in perpetuity." It also meant that Panama would remain an occupied country until it could renegotiate the despised Hay-Bunau-Varilla treaty—and renegotiation would take 74 years to achieve.

DISRUPTION AND INTERVENTION

During construction of the canal, the United States had imported tens of thousands more laborers from the West Indies, further exacerbating problems among Panama's urban poor. Panamanian landlords charged workers as much as they could get away with, and, when workers rebelled, canal officials worked with Panamanian police to quell the uprising. Three monumental renter's strikes— 1920, 1925, and 1932—accentuated the deteriorating relationship that existed between wealthy Panamanians, their American patrons, and Panama's working poor.

DÉJÀ VU

The construction of the Panama Canal resulted in the largest presence of foreign troops ever to occupy Panamanian soil. In a broader sense, however, the canal did not change the relationship between Panama's elite and its foreign patron. After independence, Amador instituted an anemic police force whose principal responsibility was election rigging, intimidating liberals during elections. As one American observer noted in 1906, "explicit directions have been given to the police to prevent by every means in their power the success of the Liberals, who, in a fair election would overthrow the Amador government by one hundred to one."[4]

Conservatives intended the new police force to serve as a mechanism of political intimidation and little else. After a protest got out of hand in 1916, the administration of President Belisario Porras permitted American officials to partially disarm the Panamanian police. Then, when protestors surround the presidential palace in 1921, President Porras asked for American troops to save his administration in the face of a massive popular protest. That same year, American troops traveled to Panama's frontier province of Chiriquí to quell political unrest there, demonstrating a shocking willingness to project the threat of military force anywhere in the republic.

The early years of the twentieth century accentuate all –too clearly the degree to which Panama's early presidents depended on foreign intervention for legitimacy. These early years also demonstrate the depths to which Panama's early politicians would stoop to remain in power, from asking foreign troops to forcibly intervene to using Panamanian police to rig election results. These practices continued, largely unabated, throughout the twentieth century. Likewise, the recruitment of additional tens of thousands of poor West Indian laborers to do the yeoman's share of canal construction badly exacerbated overcrowding and substandard living conditions in the working-class neighborhoods of Panama City and Colón.

Significant changes did occur, though, that merit mentioning here. The huge population of urban poor gradually developed a collective class conscience that made their demands and protestations much more numerically significant. In the late 1910s and throughout the 1920s, various unions took shape in these working-class neighborhoods, adding much-needed focus and breadth to Panama's urban poor. Eventually, these unions worked to ensure that Panama's workers would have a voice in the nation's government; this was particularly true in the 1970s, when the regime of General Omar Torrijos co-opted the urban worker into a broad-based popular political front to effectively challenge Panama's political and economic elite.

Also in the 1910s, 1920s, and 1930s, Panama's middle class grew rapidly because the canal greatly expanded the need for Panama's service-sector economy. This expanding middle class split over the issue of the vast American presence in their homeland. Merchants and others whose fortunes hinged on the American presence favored accommodating American interests and concerns, a group known in Panama as *rabiblancos* ("white tails"), a derogatory phrase in Panama used to describe wealthy- and middle-class Panamanians who favored the American presence because it brought them money. Conversely, various groups of white-collar professionals formed the corps of a nationalist, anti-American block whose voice grew increasingly influential in the 1930s. These nationalists grew in influence in 1935 when President Harmodio Arias founded the *Universidad de Panamá* to "preserve the Panamanian nationality."

CIVIL DISOBEDIENCE

Beginning in the 1940s, civic and political organizations that grew among Panama's poor and its expanding middle class came increasingly to jeopardize elite interests. Beginning in the 1930s, during Roosevelt's "Good Neighbor" program, presidents had taken steps to modernize Panama's police and to make it a formidable force that could effectively reckon with civil disobedience and political opposition. Consequently, when public protests and political gatherings became more common in the 1940s, Panama's governing elite used armed intimidation to quell opposition to their polices, exactly as had Somoza in Nicaragua, Carías in Honduras, Hernández Martínez in El Salvador, and Ubico in Guatemala.

Relations between Panama's ruling oligarchy and the rest of the nation's population reached a definitive boiling point in December 1947. Shortly after Pearl Harbor, Panama granted the United States permission to occupy 134 bases *outside* the Canal Zone to more effectively defend approaches to the canal. Approximately 60,000 American soldiers occupied all of Panama for the duration of the war. Given the circumstances, Panamanians generally tolerated the imposition; they had witnessed at Pearl Harbor what could happen during an enemy attack, so opposition to the expanded American military presence remained muted until the end of the war.

At war's end, politicians in Panama City and Washington dragged their feet and did not comply with the terminal clause of the treaty, which required U.S. forces to abandon these 134 additional bases within one year after the cessation of hostilities—or September 1946. American officials had no intention of complying with this last clause of the accord. In the last days of September 1946, American officials petitioned permission from Panama to remain on these additional sites, and Panamanian government officials took the petition under consideration, setting off a storm of popular protests across the Isthmus.

Panama's president, Enrique Jiménez, had a considerable sum of money invested in Panama's beef industry. The commander of Panama's National Police, José Antonio Remón Cantera, also had a significant investment in the nation's beef industry, and both Jiménez and Remón stood to lose a lot of money if the troops withdrew. Secretly, the two sides even considered "faking" a withdrawal, after which Panama's government could request their "urgent return," thus placating the opposition without losing any money.

At issue here was whether or not a Panamanian president could disregard widespread popular opposition as long as he had police support. On December 10, 1947, the Panamanian government approved the Filós-Hines Treaty, which allowed U.S. forces to remain on these 134 additional bases *despite* unprecedented opposition. Over the course of the next two weeks, a series of pitched battles occurred between tens of thousands of Panama City protestors and Remón's police, who shot indiscriminately into crowds in an effort to disperse protestors.

Jiménez's heavy-handedness and naked greed accomplished something that years of union activity and political activism had failed to accomplish; the government's glaring disregard for its constituency and the ruthlessness of the police bound together disparate groups of protestors who suddenly all had the same objective. The reversal of the Filós-Hines accord provided a rallying cry that tens of thousands of Panamanians embraced. The result was stunning. On December 22, 1947, Panama's legislative assembly unanimously rejected the Filós-Hines Treaty and required American troops to evacuate all 134 sites outside the Canal Zone.

The Filós-Hines Treaty marked a turning point in modern Panamanian history. For the first time, massive, cohesive protests had prevented Panama's governing elite from legislating in the face of popular opposition. Unquestionably, the showdown over the base issue marked a significant victory for Panamanian nationalists including students, civic groups, women's' organizations, political parties, and labor unions. In the long run, however, the confrontation over the bases issue also strengthened the role of the National Police. Believing the opposition to have been Communist-motivated and directed from Moscow, Commander Remón accelerated the professionalization of the National Police, which quickly emerged as the most powerful political arbiter on the Isthmus. In one brief period in 1949, Remón blatantly intimidated the nation's electoral board into changing its findings, and under Remón's watchful eye, Panama had three interim presidents in five days. Remón the police commander had become Remón the kingmaker, a transition that hinged in part on his refusal to allow a repeat of the "Communist-inspired" events of December, 1947.

In 1952, Remón left the police and ran successfully for president. He changed its name from the National Police to the National Guard and took a number of steps to improve the standard of living for the nation's armed force. He hired from among minorities (something previously uncommon) and built a modern *Comandancia* (police headquarters) in the Panama City working-class neighborhood of El Chorillo. The new *Comandancia* (same building destroyed in the 1989 invasion; the Guard was still head-quartered there) had a store where troops could purchase goods at reduced prices.

Remón was assassinated in 1955 while attending a horse race on the outskirts of Panama City; however, his legacy lives on. Remón was Panama's first twentieth-century military dictator. After his assassination, his successor assumed a less prominent role in the nation's military affairs. For 13 years, the National Guard "remained in its barracks," serving the whims of the political elite from the sidelines. In 1968, this calm was broken when Arnulfo Arias became president of Panama. Immediately after he took office on October 1, Arias began forcibly retiring military officers and generally meddling in the affairs of the National Guard, something he had vowed not to do. Ten days later, while Arias was viewing a movie in a downtown cinema, officers of the National Guard occupied the palace, cut off television and radio stations, and ousted Arias. On learning of this turn of events, Arias made his way along back roads to the Panama Canal Zone, where he sought asylum.

NOTES

1. Even at the onset of the twenty-first century, church and civil records capture this small oligarchy's influence: 250 years after the reforms drove them from the city, much of Panama's interior heartland remains predominantly Hispanic, with very small numbers of indigenous and Black residents in the provinces of Coclé, Herrera, Los Santos, and Veraguas.

2. Godin de Lépinay was Nicholas Joseph Adolphe Godin de Lépinay, Baron of Brusly and chief engineer with the Corps des Ponts et Chaussées (French Department of Bridges ad Highways).

3. Colón replaced Portobelo as the Atlantic port of transit at the time of construction of the Panama Railroad.

4. This is a comment made by former New York City police officer George W. Jiménez, who had been hired by Amador to train Panama's new police force.

5

The United States and Central America

In the last years of the twentieth century, the U.S. controlling interest in Central America seemed to be coming to an end. In 1989, thousands of U.S. troops invaded Panama, but 10 short years later, all U.S. military personnel withdrew from Panama. The end of the cold war in 1991 coincided with lessening tensions in El Salvador, Guatemala, and Honduras. Meanwhile, increased unrest in the Middle East shifted U.S. attention from cold war battlefields to Middle Eastern despots and terrorists. Gone were the days when hundreds of U.S. troops trained and accompanied Central American troops on missions aimed at neutralizing Soviet and Cuban sympathizers. By 2000, U.S. relations with the seven Central American republics revolved largely around trade, tourism, student exchanges, and narcotics interdiction.

The relative peace that existed in 2000 stood in stark contrast to much of the previous century, a period marked by frequent U.S. military interventions and diplomatic meddling. How did this change occur? Why is the U.S seemingly less inclined to meddle and send in troops than at anytime in the last 100 years? What does this change tell us about the future of U.S.-Central American relations?

Over the course of the twentieth century, each of the seven Central American republics and the United States experienced dramatic changes that changed perceptions, priorities, and alliances. In the early 1900s, the United States achieved significant financial influence in Central America, and World War I multiplied this influence. By the late 1920s, the United States was the primary exporter of goods to central America and the primary importer of Central American goods, giving U.S. politicians and financiers enormous influence among Central American heads of state. When the Great Depression threatened our Central American allies, the United States changed its policy to match circumstances and problems caused by the Depression; this is when U.S. policymakers decided that, in terms of diplomatic policy, the ends justify the means. It would support any government that would ally itself with the United States and against communism. Finally, during the cold war, the United States provided weapons and training in an attempt to bolster its allies' ability to defeat the Communist menace.

To understand the dynamic relationship between the United States and Central America that evolved during the twentieth century, this chapter focuses specifically on the phases of that relationship. First, a look at the late nineteenth and early twentieth centuries can explain how the United States became the dominant financial and political force in all of Central America. From there, the chapter looks at the period from the 1920s to the 1940s, a painful period for U.S. policymakers who were trying to line up their lofty pro-democracy rhetoric with the realities of economic hard times, Communist expansion, and world war. The chapter concludes by looking at the cold war and two specific forms of violent repression that emerged in Central America, both with the support and assistance of the U.S. government.

EXPANDING U.S. INFLUENCE

Throughout the nineteenth century, British financiers dominated world trade and financial markets, including much of Central and South America. Yet, by the last years of the nineteenth century, the Industrial Revolution had transformed the United States into a world-class importer and exporter of manufactured goods. This rapid progress became most obvious in the Central American financial sector, where the United States caught and surpassed

Table 5.1 United States Trade with all Central American Republics: Import/Export Percentages

Country	1909	1910	1911	1912	1913	1914
Costa Rica	51/59	39/60	46/55	58/50	51/51	53/45
El Salvador	32/29	36/31	35/33	37/30	40/29	41/25
Guatemala	42/27	n/a	41/30	46/29	50/27	52/38
Honduras	69/88	68/82	71/89	67/88	67/87	79/87
Nicaragua	52/42	55/34	48/31	51/46	56/35	62/49
Panama	—/—	56/85	54/84	55/86	55/86	65/86

Table 5.2 Country-by-Country Trade with Central American Republics: Import/Export Percentages, 1909–1914

Country	1909	1910	1911	1912	1913	1914
United States	49/49	50/52	48/48	52/49	53/46	58/49
England	22/15	21/15	20/13	18/15	18/14	16/15
France	5/9	5/10	5/13	5/7	5/9	4/8
Germany	14/19	11/12	15/25	14/21	14/21	12/17

their British and European counterparts. By the end of the century, the United States controlled both import and export markets for all the Central American republics (Tables 5.1 and 5.2).

The U.S. domination of the Central American markets before World War I gave American financiers and politicians an important advantage as the war began. Financially and politically, the United States wished to eliminate European influence in the Western Hemisphere, and they could accomplish this by purchasing British, German, and French holdings in public utilities, transportation, and industry in Central America. American financiers gained control of the Central American economies as the twentieth century dawned.

As its financial influence in Central America expanded, the United States became increasingly bold in its relations with the nations of Central America and the Caribbean. When Colombia refused to agree to U.S. requests to build a canal across Panama, President Roosevelt "took" Panama with military force and secured that nation's independence from Colombia on November 3, 1903. On November 18, the Roosevelt administration got the new Panamanian government to agree to a treaty, allowing the United States to build a canal across the newly independent nation.

In his 1904 Corollary to the Monroe Doctrine, President Theodore Roosevelt warned the nations of Central America and the Caribbean to behave themselves or face American military might:

> Any country whose people conduct themselves well can count upon our hearty friendship. If a nation shows that it knows how to act with reasonable efficiency and decency in social and political matters, if it keeps order and pays its obligations, it need fear no interference from the United States. Chronic wrongdoing, or an impotence which results in a general loosening of the ties of civilized society, may in America, as elsewhere, ultimately require intervention by some civilized nation, and in the Western Hemisphere the adherence of the United States to the Monroe Doctrine may lead the United States, however reluctantly, in flagrant cases of such wrongdoing or impotence, to the exercise of an international police power ... We would interfere with them only in the last resort, and then only if it became evident that their inability or unwillingness to do justice at home and abroad had violated the rights of the United States or had invited foreign aggression to the detriment of the entire body of American nations.

In 1907, the United States appeared to back off the aggressive language of the Roosevelt Corollary. That year the governments of Costa Rica, El Salvador, Guatemala, Honduras, and Nicaragua convened a conference on Central American affairs in Washington and invited the United States to attend as an honorary participant. During this conference the five Central America nations drafted a "General Treaty of Peace and Amity" and invited the United States to sign, to which the American diplomats quickly agreed.

This treaty called on participants to refuse diplomatic recognition to any government that came to power through illegal means: military revolt, political intrigue, or foreign intervention. In theory the agreement was a forceful statement in favor of democratic government, and U.S. involvement seemed to provide powerful reinforcement for the principles outlined. In practice the United States repeatedly violated the 1907 agreement, thus rendering it meaningless. In 1909, for example, 400 American marines landed in Nicaragua and helped pressure liberal President José Santos Zelaya to resign under pressure in December 1909. Zelaya's successor, José Madriz, was also a liberal and was also pressured into resigning the next year. American troops continued to intervene in Nicaraguan politics until their withdrawal in 1933.

The military occupation of Nicaragua by U.S. marines in 1909 marked the beginning of a new period in Central American history, one in which U.S. influence grew increasingly prevalent. As U.S. influence increased in the 1910s and 1920s, politicians in Central American countries had to deal progressively more with American policies and the whims of the U.S. economy, where demand for Central American goods was growing increasingly decisive for the Central American republics. In Honduras, for example, the Vacarro brothers of New Orleans established brisk trade in Honduran bananas, shipping hundreds of tons of bananas from Honduras to New Orleans. Their company, Standard Fruit, expanded quickly and played a pivotal role in Honduran politics. Standard and other American fruit companies gained favorable contracts and lucrative tax breaks.

Gradually, the success of Honduran presidents came to depend in part on how well they related with Standard Fruit and other foreign companies. The Vacarro brothers had begun to export Honduran bananas to the United States in 1899, and soon thereafter railroad construction revolved around Standard's need to get bananas to market. In 1903, General Manuel Bonilla overthrew the administration of General Terencio Sierra. Bonilla, a close friend of the fruit companies, benefited from this relationship. He jailed his political enemies while granting U.S. fruit companies tax exemptions and permission to build port facilities and railroads in exchange for their support of his government's policies.

WORLD WAR I: BEGINNING OF THE "AMERICAN ERA"

World War I marked a turning point in U.S.-Central American relations. As the war erupted in Europe, Britain still dominated the world's economic markets. Industrialization had made England very rich, and since the beginning of the Industrial Revolution, London had been the center of the world's financial sectors—the Wall Street of the nineteenth century; however, World War I drastically redistributed the world's wealth. By 1917, the British, French, and German governments had spent their reserves almost entirely

Table 5.3 Average Annual Cost of World War I as a Percentage of National Income

United States	England	France	Germany
15.5%	36.92%	25.59%	31.58%

Table 5.4 National Debts of the United States, England, France, and Germany: 1912–1916 in U.S. Dollars

Years	United States	England	France	Germany
1912–1914	$1,027,574,697	$3,479,070,854	$6,343,622,400	$4,538,654,400
1916	$1,132,639,195	$17,336,000,000	$18,005,000,000	$16,978,000,000

Table 5.5 Per Capita Debt of the United States, England, France, and Germany: 1912–1916 in U.S. Dollars

Years	United States	England	France	Germany
1912–1914	$10.76	$76.19	$159.95	$73.62
1916	$10.56	$382	$455	$255

on the war, shipping large quantities of their cash and gold to the United States to pay for weapons, munitions, and myriad other supplies (Table 5.3). The war proved devastating to the European economies. Both the Allied Forces and the Central Powers exhausted their national gold reserves on war items, quickly becoming debtor nations in the process.

World War I had exactly the opposite effect on the U.S. economy: the war made the United States a creditor nation. The United States did not officially enter the conflict until it was more than half over. In the meantime, it had been supplying the Allied Forces with weapons, ammunition, food, and medical supplies. Payment for these wartime goods introduced large portions of European gold and capital reserves into the U.S. economy (these transitions in the economies of the United States,

Table 5.6 Change in United States Investments in Central America for the Years 1913 and 1929

Costa Rica	El Salvador	Guatemala	Honduras	Nicaragua	Panama
+80%	+80%	+48%	+77%	+88%	+25%

Great Britain, France, and Germany are graphically displayed in terms of growing national debt in Tables 5.4 and 5.5. Consequently, as Europe's capital reserves dried up during the course of the war, the United States became the world's chief financial center in the span of four years, replacing Britain as the world's banker.

The economic influence of World War I on the world's financial centers was critical to Central American development because this sudden increase in capital reserves meant increased lending power for investors in the United States, and Americans now moved to control the evasive Central American bonds and securities markets. At the same time, the British and European nations now had insufficient assets to resist the American move (Table 5.5). In the years after the war, financial speculators in the United States "bought out" British and European interests in Central America, effectively reducing Europe's influence in the region while securing for themselves enormous influence (Table 5.6). In 1921, John Foster Bass and Harold Glenn Moulton, two American economists, noted that:

> It will be recalled that the great increase in exports from the United States, as well as from neutral countries, resulted (1) in shifting a disproportionate quantity of the gold supply of the world to the United States; (2) in the resale to the United States of European investments in American securities; and (3) in the creation of huge foreign debts to the United States.[1]

By controlling Central America's imports and exports, U.S. markets played a decisive role in determining what Central Americans would and would not consume, as well as what they would and would not produce. After the war, Americans controlled Central America's banks, customs houses, public utilities, public works projects, railroads, and ports.

THE 1907 TREATY REVISITED: "DISINTERESTED THOUGHTFULNESS"

After more than a decade wherein U.S. troops and companies repeatedly violated the 1907 General Treaty of Peace and Amity, the Central American republics again arranged a convention in Washington in 1923. As they had in 1907, Central Americans once again invited the United States to participate. Once again, diplomats from Costa Rica, El Salvador, Guatemala, Honduras, and Nicaragua attended. Once again, the conference produced a General Treaty of Peace and Amity wherein the signatories agreed to deny diplomatic recognition to any government that rose to power through other than legal means. And once again, the United States was invited to sign the treaty. Guatemalan Minister Francísco Sánchez Latour even lauded the U.S.'s "disinterested thoughtfulness" with regard to Central America.

The 1923 treaty reaffirmed the principal tenets of the defunct 1907 agreement. The six signers agreed not to grant diplomatic recognition to governments that came to power illegally through military force, electoral fraud, or foreign intervention. By isolating political opportunists in this fashion, participants hoped to prevent political chicanery and to ensure political stability. During the next several years the policy worked. In 1923, the United States joined its Central American allies in refusing to recognize the government of Tiburcio Carías Andino (future dictator of Honduras). In 1930, the United States and its Central American allies withheld recognition from General Manuel Orellana of Guatemala, who "compelled" President Baudilla Palma to resign and then assumed the presidency himself.

Despite U.S. adherence to the 1923 accord throughout the remainder of the 1920s, U.S. officials began to reconsider their options in Central America as a result of rapidly changing circumstances at the end of the decade. The General Treaty of Peace and Amity had been a bold statement in support of representative government. At the time of the 1923 conference, economies and politics in Central America remained relatively stable. Worker unrest remained insignificant compared with that of other decades, and Central American heads of state kept that unrest in check. Once the Great Depression began affecting Central American markets and governments, however, the United States faced a difficult choice: if popularly elected heads of state in Central America cannot control worker unrest in order to preserve political stability, is it best to continue supporting the government? Or should the United States instead support a military dictator who violates the 1923 agreement but who is able to maintain order and political stability?

As the decade of the 1930s began and workers responded to difficulties of life during the Depression, the extreme poverty of Central America would provide a laboratory where the United States would test this difficult equation. Its conclusion—that the "end" of preventing communist infiltration justified whatever "means" might be necessary in Central America including doing business with brutal military dictators—would shape U.S. policy toward Central America throughout much of the remainder of the twentieth century.

DICTATORS, BLOODSHED, AND POLICY DRIFT

The Great Depression marked a turning point in U.S. policy toward Central America. The financial crisis affected working-class Central Americans first and most severely. Anti-American and anticapitalist movements developed among tens of thousands of workers who had grown tired of their oppressive work and living circumstances. In response to increasing protests, Central America's wealthy found the answer to their dilemma in military dictators who were strong enough militarily to impose rule on the restless workers.

This new period of violent political repression began in Guatemala where General Jorge Ubico, elected in 1931, executed large numbers of communists, along with thousands of Indians. During his first three years in office, his merciless violence nearly eliminated the Guatemalan Communist Party. At the height of Ubico's dictatorship, President Franklin D. Roosevelt sent Ubico a personal letter to congratulate him for remaining in office (although continuing in office was in direct violation of the Guatemalan constitution), and State Department officials were exuberant over the fact that in Ubico, the United States had a friend willing to "devote his labor to the maintenance and consolidation of the cordial relations which happily exist between the United States and Guatemala."

In 1932, politicians and the wealthy of El Salvador and Honduras took similar steps to resolve their political problems. General Hernández Martínez (El Salvador) and Tiburcio Carías Andino (Honduras) consolidated dictatorial powers with which to rule their respective countries, and in the process they gained the support of both the United States and the landed elite of their respective countries by viciously suppressing liberals and communists.

As had occurred in the case of Ubico in Guatemala, when Hernández Martínez announced his intention to "extend" the period of his presidency, his decision received support from the United States despite the accords of 1907 and 1923. When Hernández Martínez sent troops to slaughter 20,000 peasants in 1932, he received the assistance, support, and appreciation of the United States. As Frank P. Corrigan, U.S. Minister in El Salvador at the time, noted in the wake of this event (known in El Salvador as *la matanza* [the slaughter]):

> The wealthiest Salvadorans and leaders of the foreign groups as well as the political job holders encourage the continuance in office of President Martínez. The foreign businessmen and wealthier Salvadorans are inspired by fear of the "menace" of communism and remember his record in that regard.

Nicaragua followed suit in 1936 by "electing" General Anastasio Somoza to the presidency. Although aware that Somoza had won a completely fraudulent election that he manipulated as the head of the country's National Guard, the United States sent an official envoy to his inauguration, granting Somoza the U.S. stamp of approval in the process.

MAKING THE ENDS JUSTIFY THE MEANS

By the mid-1930s, the United States found itself in a difficult predicament regarding Central America. On the one hand, U.S. officials had sanctimoniously and regularly declared their preference for democracy and representative government in Central America and elsewhere. On the other hand, the dictatorships of Hernández Martínez (El Salvador), Tiburcio Carías Andino (Honduras), Jorge Ubico (Guatemala), and Anastasio Somoza (Nicaragua) used armed violence to control worker unrest and peasant disruptions. Despite the unattractive appearance of allying with brutal dictators, U.S. officials believed stability and security outweighed any concerns Americans may have entertained regarding their new-found allies. Put another way, the ends (peace and stability) justified the means (violent repression and death).

In the late 1920s and early 1930s, world circumstances had changed dramatically in unpredictable ways. Financial difficulties caused by the Depression spawned unrest among Central America's poor, who increasingly resented and protested their circumstances. Central America's politicians and its wealthy answered this unrest with violent repression, drawing their nations' militaries into the fray to an extent unprecedented in their histories. Forced by circumstances to decide which side to support, the United States chose to assist and support anyone with enough power to control the unrest. This is how the United States became close allies and supporters of brutal military dictators in Central America. This "means-to-an-end" diplomacy would dominate U.S. policy toward Central America for the remainder of the twentieth century.

Recognizing this dilemma, U.S. State Department officials began considering how best to opt out of the 1923 treaty. Of particular concern was how to grant recognition to Anastasio Somoza of Nicaragua, where U.S. citizens had extensive financial interests. As the United States pondered how best to gracefully abandon the 1923 accord and grant recognition and support to Somoza, one State Department official reasoned in 1935 that:

> ... we are no longer warranted in invoking the [1923] Treaty as a reason for denying recognition to any régime in Central America, since we (who are not even party to the Treaty) cannot justly invoke it in the case of one violation when the Parties to it themselves have both violated it and failed to invoke it in the cases of other and previous violations. To endeavor to do so would be arbitrary and capricious and would constitute "meddling" of a flagrant kind.

Amazingly, this statement reflects the fact that over the course of 12 years, U.S. officials had decided that (1) the United States was not even a party to the treaty, and (2) to *refuse* to recognize a dictator by invoking the 1923 treaty would actually constitute "flagrant ... meddling."

In the name of "stability," the United States announced a new agreement that better fit U.S. preferences: the 1936 Defensive Alliance Against Communism. This new relationship hinged on the U.S. belief that ends justify means in diplomacy and that they needed to side with whomever could protect American interests. Under the 1936 pronouncement, the United States no longer considered itself bound by democratic parameters when dealing with

Central America. Elected governments had proven incapable of defending the region against "latent communism," and now for the first time the State Department conceded publicly that, regardless of what indiscretions they committed (i.e., Hernández Martínez and his 1932 *matanza*), the United States preferred to work with dictators rather than with representative governments.

Beyond making a mockery of Central American efforts to maintain peace, U.S. policy shifts in the 1910s, 1920s, and 1930s divided Central Americans into two groups: those who favored a decisive U.S. presence in their respective countries versus those who resented foreign intervention in their nations' affairs. Moreover, by encouraging the use of violent repression to maintain order, the United States simplistically divided Central Americans into neat, easy-to-understand ideological camps: "free" and "communist." Finally, by working with unsavory dictatorships in the name of "stability," the United States provided political legitimacy to a generation of despots who would not have achieved political prominence without Washington's favor. General Hernández Martínez Martínez provided a transparent example of this phenomenon.

LEND LEASE

The Great Depression caused the United States to change its priorities in its relations with Central America. Unrest among the poor in Central America seemed to provide a breeding ground for communism in the Americas. By allying themselves with ruthless dictators in Central America, U.S. politicians, statesmen, and financiers believed they helped stop the spread of communism while making the region safe for American interests.

In the 1940s, dramatic, rapidly changing circumstances once again caused the United States to reconsider its relationship with Central America. After Japan's attack on Pearl Harbor, it appeared that our dictator allies would need significant assistance to fend off Japanese and German aggression. In the Canal Zone, American officials kept close track of every Japanese, Italian, and German citizen living in and around Panama City. Regular military reports monitored the movements and actions of each of these hundreds of individuals.

Outside Panama, U.S. officials had to find other ways to shore up Central American defenses. In the months after the attack on Pearl Harbor, German U-boats sank more than 200 ships in the Atlantic, and U.S. military and government officials worried about the possibility of enemy infiltration in Central America; they also worried about the vulnerability of the Panama Canal, still a vital waterway in American military strategy.

On March 21, 1942, President Roosevelt's government enacted the Lend-Lease program, which logically gave priority to supporting Great Britain and our other European allies. In Central America, Lend-Lease assistance was given in exchange for military cooperation and the use of various strategic bases and ports throughout the region. Throughout the remainder of World War II, the United States used Lend-Lease to provide $400 million in war materials to the Latin American republics including Central America. These materials included weapons, ammunition, armor, training, and other supplies. This amount pales when compared to the billions of U.S. dollars given to our European allies, but the amount provided a staggering amount of aid for the small Central American nations. The military dictatorships aligned with the United States before the war received tanks, armored personnel carriers, guns, munitions of all types, and superb training by U.S. military specialists.

These weapons and this training were never used against the Axis powers during World War II. Instead, when the war ended Central American military commanders possessed advanced weapons and training to fight—but no enemy. The feared invasion and exploitation of Central America never came, and many of the weapons and all of the training Central American militaries had received from the United States remained in the respective nations' arsenals. The U.S. Central American allies emerged from the war better equipped than ever before to repress opposition to government policies. Throughout the next five decades, dictators in the various Central American republics would use U.S. World War II-era tanks, aircraft, personnel carriers, and light weapons to crush peasant rebellions and labor unrest while brutally suppressing political enemies.

THE BEGINNINGS OF THE COLD WAR

When World War II concluded, the United States sought to retain its wartime influence in Central America. Because the United States controlled the 500 square mile-Canal Zone in Panama, Pentagon officials decided to locate its permanent training facilities inside the Canal Zone. Founded in 1946 as the Latin American Training

Center, the new school was located at Fort Amador in the Panama Canal Zone. Four years later the school was renamed the U.S. Army Caribbean School. U.S. military officials moved the school to Fort Gulick and made Spanish the school's official language. At this new school, U.S. troops could carefully control access to the school and its students.

At the U.S. Army Caribbean School, U.S. soldiers taught Central American soldiers (in Spanish) survival and combat techniques, reconnaissance techniques, weapons systems, vehicle maintenance, etc. This training forged a lasting relationship between Central America's militaries and the U.S. government, which had a vested interest in the success of the training program. In the months and years after World War II ended, increased professionalism among Central American soldiers would improve their ability to thwart peasant unrest, now viewed by the United States as the ideal breeding ground for the spread of communism.

In July 1963, the Kennedy administration renamed the school, calling it the School of the Americas (SOA). Central American soldiers arrived in Panama by the hundreds to be trained by U.S. military personnel, who were now joined by U.S. intelligence personnel. U.S. policymakers had grown increasingly interested in counterinsurgency tactics because of the unconventional guerilla warfare conflict in Vietnam, so counterinsurgency became another staple of the SOA curriculum. Soldiers trained at the SOA learned how to fight, how to keep themselves alive, how to maintain their equipment, how to evade capture, and how to interrogate prisoners and extract sensitive information from them.

As a result of the Panama Canal treaties, the SOA relocated to Fort Benning, Georgia, in 1984. At Fort Benning the school continued training thousands of Central American troops in advanced military tactics regarding everything from crowd control to protest disbursement and counterinsurgency. Not long after its relocation, the SOA began to come under intense public opposition. Despite the school's stated mission, "the promotion of democracy, institutional accountability to civilian authority, and transparency and cooperation between the militaries of the hemisphere," evidence in the late 1970s and 1980s suggested that Central American graduates of the SOA were using their training to violate human rights in their home countries.[2]

GOVERNMENT-SPONSORED TERRORISM: DEATH SQUADS

During the cold war each of the nations of Central America experienced periods of economic upheaval and political unrest. Of the seven Central American republics, only Belize and Costa Rica escaped extended periods of government-sponsored violence against their respective civilian populations. Of the other five nations, three experienced widespread worker unrest crushed by government-sponsored *escuadrones de la muerte* (death squads): El Salvador, Guatemala, and Honduras. These "informal" paramilitary units, normally consisting of off-duty soldiers, proved brutally efficient and merciless. In the 1970s and 1980s, the dictatorships in these three countries killed more than 100,000 peasants in their struggle against "communism." Considered "freedom fighters" by many in the United States, officers and soldiers in these death squads frequently received their training from the SOA.

Conversely, in Nicaragua and Panama the close relationship between each nation's military dictatorship and Washington bred a more "formal" type of political repression in which active-duty soldiers (National Guard) would do the dictatorship's political bidding. These formal killing machines proved no less merciless than their informal counterparts elsewhere in Central America; in Nicaragua in the 1970s, the Somoza regime wiped out entire villages using World War II-era U.S. military hardware.

DEATH SQUAD ACTIVITY DURING THE COLD WAR

To understand why the United States would collaborate with death squads and other terrorists, one must understand the tense and fearsome nature of the cold war. Much was at stake, possibly the very existence of the world, and the United States played aggressively. In March 1985, President Ronald Reagan summed up these concerns in a speech he gave to representatives from various Central American republics when they visited him in the White House:

> But the Soviet Union has its own plan for Central America, a region which Soviet Foreign Minister Gromyko described as "boiling like a cauldron." In the last 5 years, the Soviets have provided more military assistance to Cuba and Nicaragua alone than the United States has provided to all of Latin America. The Soviets' plan is designed to crush self-determination of free people, to crush democracy in

Costa Rica, Honduras, El Salvador, Guatemala, and Panama. It's a plan to turn Central America into a Soviet beachhead of aggression that could spread terror and instability north and south, disrupt our vital sea lanes, cripple our ability to carry out our commitments to our European allies, and send tens of millions of refugees streaming in a human tidal wave across all our borders.

This is the premise that underlies U.S. support of governments that sometimes do terrible things; it is the "end" that justified any steps we might take—any allies we might support—to prevent the establishment of a "Soviet beachhead of aggression." In the process we also helped terrorize tens of thousands of civilians, many of whom were neither "Soviet" nor "American." They were simply caught in the middle of a cold war battlefield.

El Salvador

The SOA's problem of public perception came to a head in the 1980s. In March 1980, Monsignor Oscar Romero, Archbishop of El Salvador, was assassinated while administering mass in a San Salvador church. The popular priest's murder sparked outrage in El Salvador and throughout Central America, and public outrage soon forced the government of El Salvador to investigate. On May 7, 1980, investigators made a significant breakthrough while raiding a house where a dozen people were meeting, including various current and former members of the Salvadoran military. Among those arrested was Roberto D'Aubuisson, a former major in the Salvadoran military and a prominent organizer of radical right-wing *escuadrones de la muerte* (death squads)—off-duty soldiers hired to eliminate political enemies of the rich. These death squads targeted labor activists, students, members of the clergy, farm workers, villages in conflict zones, and members of various political parties deemed to be at odds with government policies.

In a 1993 report, the United Nations Truth Commission on El Salvador concluded, "There is full evidence that former major Roberto D'Aubuisson gave the order to assassinate the Archbishop and gave precise instructions to members of his security service, acting as a death squad, to organize and supervise the assassination." Like many other Salvadoran officers, D'Aubuisson was a graduate of the SOA where he had been trained in intelligence and counterintelligence in early 1970.[3]

The assassins and their accomplices escaped justice with the help of the governments of El Salvador and the United States. The government of El Salvador issued an amnesty law in 1993 for the principal officers involved in Romero's murder. Other accomplices found alternative means of avoiding justice. For example, former Salvadoran Air Force officer Alvaro Rafael Saravia, D'Aubuisson's assistant, had actually arranged Archbishop Romero's murder for D'Aubuisson and paid the assassin. In 1987, Saravia fled to the United States, moving around and ultimately settling in Modesto, California. Saravia lived in Modesto and worked as a used car salesman until mid-2004, when a judge in California brought charges against him for Romero's murder and for crimes against humanity. Saravia went into hiding and has not been seen since; the U.S. Immigration and Customs Service has sought him since his disappearance.

D'Aubuisson himself repeatedly denied having any part in the archbishop's murder, at one point blaming a leftist rebel for the murder, until it was learned that the rebel had been in prison at the time of the murder. D'Aubuisson formed a reactionary anti-Communist political party, the *Alianza Republicana Nacionalista* (ARENA) (the Nationalist Republican Alliance), in 1981. Because of his extreme anti-Communist policies D'Aubuisson enjoyed the support of much of El Salvador's wealthy and middle class. ARENA has dominated Salvadoran politics since its founding. Meanwhile, D'Aubuisson died in 1992 a free man and a powerful political force in El Salvador.

Archbishop Romero's murder marked the escalation of violence in El Salvador. On December 2, 1980, four American nuns (Maryknoll Sisters) were murdered by members of El Salvador's National Guard. During the next 10 years, El Salvador's military massacred entire villages, killed students and priests, and violently repressed government opponents, frequently raping, torturing, and murdering large numbers of people. When the United Nations Truth Commission investigated El Salvador's problems and issued its findings in 1993, it identified the officers responsible for these multiple crimes against humanity. Two thirds of those named by the United Nations had graduated from the SOA.

Guatemala

Since the mid-1950s, Guatemala's majority indigenous population has struggled to survive, often confronting government death squads intent on eliminating entire villages. In 2000, Maya spokes-woman Rigoberta Menchú filed suit against former president, General Efrain Rios Montt, charging him with mass murder and attempted genocide against that nation's large indigenous popula-tion. Rios Montt, an SOA graduate, took power in a military coup at the height of a bloody counterinsurgency campaign in the 1980s. During Rios Montt's presidency, hundreds of Mayan villages were eliminated, tens of thousands of Indians were slaughtered, and hundreds of thousands of peasants became homeless.

In a similar case, a group of Mayan survivors sued various former Guatemalan military chiefs, including former Army Chief of Staff Benedicto Lucas Garciá, accusing them of ordering the rape, torture, and slaughter of entire Mayan villages. García, an SOA graduate, was the principal architect of the Guatemalan army's scorched-earth plan to eliminate Guatemala's Mayan population.

For five decades, the U.S. government officially denied any role in Guatemala's 1954 counter-revolution and subsequent civil war against that nation's large Mayan population. Then, in May 2003, the U.S. Department of State issued a retrospective account of the 1954 crisis wherein the United States officially acknowledged its role in the violent ouster of that nation's democratically elected president, Jacobo Arbenz.

Honduras

In Honduras, military officers used a death squad format similar to that used in El Salvador to eliminate opponents of the govern-ment. General Gustavo Alvarez Martínez and his peer, General Daniel Bali Castillo, both took a Joint Operations course at the SOA in 1978. On returning to Honduras, Alavarez Martínez and Bali Castillo established Battalion 3–16, the infamous military unit that provided soldiers and training for death squad activities in Honduras in the 1980s. Nineteen key members of the brutal Battalion 3–16 graduated from the SOA, and these leaders used their training and weapons to rape, torture, and kill opponents of the government. Long after the Americas Watch group identi-fied these men for their crimes against humanity, some returned to SOA for additional training and even to serve as guest speakers.

From 1981 to 1985, John Negroponte served as U.S. ambassador to Honduras. During his ambassadorship, Negroponte oversaw a large embassy staff and interacted closely with one of the largest Central Intelligence Agency stations anywhere in the world. This was the height of the Communist regime in Nicaragua, and, under Negroponte's watchful eye, the United States used Honduras as a staging lane to fight the Communist Sandinistas. During this period, U.S. military assistance to Honduras increased from $3.9 million to $77.4 million.

This funding and the large U.S. military and intelligence missions in Honduras provided critical support for Battalion 3–16 and other Honduran military units who violently repressed opposition to the government while also crushing support inside Honduras for the Nicaraguan Communists.

Nicaragua

The government of Nicaragua formally relied on National Guard soldiers rather than death squads to do its political bidding. The Somoza dictatorship enjoyed more direct support from the United States than perhaps any other government in the Americas, and the Somozas put this U.S. support to good use. After fraudulently ascending to the presidency in 1936, Somoza also gained control of the nation's legislature and its judiciary, giving the Somoza family unprecedented total control of all facets of government in Nicaragua.

Somoza achieved this most comprehensive of all dictatorships by using the National Guard to intimidate and violently repress any opposition to him and his family. With the help of weapons and support from the United States, Somoza's National Guard violently thwarted serious political opposition and antigovernment demonstrations. Under Somoza's control, the institutional power of the National Guard grew in most government-owned enterprises until eventually it controlled the national radio and telegraph networks, the postal and immigration services, health services, the internal revenue service, and the national railroads. Put another way. Somoza controlled the National Guard, which controlled much of the rest of the country. This reality made Somoza a perfect ally for the United States; in times of peace and war, Somoza and his sons succeeded in maintaining strict order in Nicaragua throughout the Somoza era (1936–1979).

The effects of the Somoza dictatorship were no less disastrous than the effects of death squads elsewhere in Central America.

Under the Somoza "kleptocracy" (government by theft—a term frequently used by scholars to describe the Somoza dynasty), the gap between rich and poor grew ever wider. Most Nicaraguans lived under the poorest of circumstances, and the Somoza government used violent repression to keep the peasant masses in check. The result was a civil war that began in the late 1970s and destroyed the nation's economy while claiming tens of thousands of lives.

Panama

Like the dictatorship in Nicaragua, the military dictatorships of Generals Omar Torrijos and Manuel Noriega used on-duty soldiers to terrorize political opponents. This formal repression actually began in the late 1940s under then-police commander José Remón, who used the National Police to terrorize government opponents. Remón had full U.S. support because he blamed Communists for political uprisings. Remón was Panama's first dictator, and by blaming Moscow for worker unrest and student problems, he had Washington's support for even the most flagrant, violent acts of repression.

It was not until October 1968, however, that a military officer overthrew a democratically elected government in Panama and made himself head of state. That month, SOA graduate Omar Torrijos overthrew the democratically elected government of Arnulfo Arias and began a military dictatorship that lasted until 1989. Torrijos did not used death squads to eliminate his political enemies, but he did use his troops to settle political disputes. An event that occurred in mid-1969 reaffirmed the Torrijos government's willingness to use lethal force and to call on the United States for help when it was needed. In mid-1969 Torrijos' National Guard uncovered an opposition cell operating in a rural mountain community of Cerro Azul (Blue Mountain). Using helicopters borrowed from the U.S. military, National Guard troops flew into the area and attacked the activists. The leaders of the movement all died at the hands of the National Guard. The Cerro Azul slaughter drove the more radical opponents of the Torrijos regime into the underground, where they used university campuses and other public areas to voice their protests.

Less radical groups in Panama found other creative ways to voice their opposition to the military regime. From 1968 to 1972, for example, a group of female activists in Panama City published and circulated a weekly protest newsletter, *El Grito*, which denounced the Torrijos government's violent repression of opponents and its reliance on the United States for military and economic support. These women paid a steep price for their patriotic fervor: several women who distributed *El Grito* had their cars confiscated, many women were stopped and intimidated by gun-toting guardsmen, and many were raped by National Guard officers.

As had been the case in El Salvador, the clergy in Panama also paid a steep price for opposing the military regime. Father Hector Gallego, a vocal critic of the Torrijos regime, was abducted and murdered by members of Panama's National Guard on the evening of June 9, 1971.

When General Torrijos died mysteriously in a July 1981 plane crash, General Manuel Noriega, another SOA graduate, quickly emerged as Panama's new military dictator. Noriega continued Torrijos' practice of violently repressing opposition. With the passage of time and the worsening of Panama's financial situation in the late-1980s, Noriega became more stridently violent than Torrijos had ever been. His ruthlessness culminated with an attempted 1989 coup against him by dozens of his junior officers. Noriega loyalists rescued their chief after several hours, capturing the rebel officers and incarcerating them. Noriega had the rebels transferred to a military post on the outskirts of Panama City, where they were tortured and executed.

CONCLUSIONS

In the years after the World War II, the United States spent billions of dollars maintaining and strengthening its relationship to the militaries and governments of Central America. U.S. military officials considered the protection and stability of the Central American republics essential for the defense of the U.S. homeland. Moreover, the U.S. Joint Chiefs of Staff considered Central America critical for the successful defense of the Panama Canal, which was still of sufficient importance to merit a U.S. military invasion in December 1989.

During the twentieth century various watershed world events sparked increased interest in Central America among U.S. policymakers. The Depression caused U.S. policymakers to reevaluate their commitment to democratic forms of government. In the wake of World War II, fear of Communist expansion prompted U.S.

officials to increase the flow of weapons and money in an attempt to stave off the establishment of "a Communist beachhead in Central America." The counterinsurgency in Vietnam further caused U.S. policymakers to consider how best to deal with Communist insurgents in tropical settings.

As world events ebbed and flowed so, too, did Washington's commitment to democracy. In times of peace democracy was to be embraced, as demonstrated by the treaties of 1907 and 1923. When economic and military hardships struck, however, pragmatic realities took precedent and U.S. policymakers pursued what they deemed prudent means of maintaining peace. In times of duress for the United States in its dealings with Central America, the ends definitely justified the means.

Even in a rapidly changing world, some things remained constant in relations between the United States and Central America. First, the United States proved willing to take whatever diplomatic steps it deemed necessary to ensure stability in Central America. Second, throughout the twentieth century, the United States repeatedly sent its own soldiers to Central America on military missions of various sorts. Sometimes U.S. troops invaded and occupied nations; other times, U.S. military missions spent time in Central America, "advising" local militaries on tactics and strategies. Third, in addition to diplomatic and military steps, the United States began training Latin American troops in the art of warfare. Over time this training evolved to meet new challenges from weapons use and survival skills to counterinsurgency training.

Along the way, a dichotomy appeared that seems difficult for the United States to comprehend. The troops being trained and armed by the United States are not returning home to defend their motherlands from foreign invaders. Instead, the evidence now clearly establishes that many of the beneficiaries of U.S. funding and training return to their own countries and use the training they received to torture, terrorize, and murder their own civilian populations.

NOTES

1. John Foster Bass and Harold Glenn Moulton, *America and the Balance Sheet in Europe* (New York: The Ronald Press, 1921), p. 301.

2. Colonel Glenn R. Weidner, Commandant, "The U.S. Army School of the Americas," mission statement located on the Internet at: http://carlisle-www.army.mil/usamhi/usarsa/COMDT/SOAREV.htm

3. For information on graduates of the School of the Americas, visit the Web site of the "School of the Americas Watch": http://www.soaw.org/new/grads_search.php. At this screen you can simply select a country and see a list of all graduates from that country.

6

The Cold War I: Communism and "Freedom Fighters"

After independence the new Central American nations faced similar challenges. A power vacuum occurred because Central Americans gained little upper-level administrative experience under the Spanish Empire. Also, the mercantilist nature of the colonial Spanish economy left them with one or two basic export commodities, rendering them extremely vulnerable to fluctuations in market demand and prices. This vulnerability most directly affected the poor, whose employment and wages ebbed and flowed with economic trends. When worker unrest led to protests and work stoppages, the governing elite turned increasingly to armed violence to thwart worker protests.

In the first decades of the twentieth century, the region's elite took the use of violence to a new level. Confronted by severe economic unrest and peasant protests in the 1920s and 1930s, the governing elite in Central America became increasingly ruthless in their use of violence to terrorize their constituencies into submission. During the 1930s and 1940s, tens of thousands of peasants were murdered by the governments of Guatemala, El Salvador, Nicaragua, and Honduras. In each instance these dictators invoked the specter of communism to court Washington's support, and generally Washington did not disappoint them.

After World War II Central America's poor gradually began responding to this military repression, triggering a cycle of violence wherein fragile peace briefly separated extended periods of increasing violence. Between 1950 and 2000, this cycle of violence claimed more than 200,000 lives and resolved little; at the onset of the twenty-first century, civil strife and ethnic unrest continue essentially unabated. Some U.S. scholars speak of "redemocratization," as if countries who previously grappled with these cycles of violence suddenly snapped out of the cycle, saw the "light," and joined together in an effort to establish representative government. In much of Central America, discussion of redemocratization is both misleading and unfounded conjecture on the region's history. To redemocratize there must first have existed a democracy.

A close look at political conditions in Central America in the years after World War II emphasizes the incessant role of violence and corruption in the region's political processes. Excepting Costa Rica, only Guatemala (1944, 1950) and Honduras (1957) held legitimate elections in the postwar era that resulted in the peaceful transfer of power. Much more common elsewhere were "preventive coups" to eliminate a political enemy and election fraud to place a veneer of legitimacy on the coup.[1]

When considering various case studies of political violence in recent Central American history, two salient underlying, common themes merit consideration. The first is the increasing sophistication of mass resistance. In the years after World War II, workers formed civic action groups, joined labor unions, and became more active in organized political parties. Despite the ongoing cycles of violence that frequently threatened their well-being, Central America's poor were eventually able to bring to bear significant peaceful pressure on their governments so as to actually affect the outcome of government decisions. Such was the case in Guatemala, for example, where in the 1980s and 1990s, peasants orchestrated a brilliant campaign against human rights abuses, ultimately focusing international attention on the problem and, for a time, stemming the violent repression that has characterized Guatemalan history since the early 1950s.

A second recurrent theme is the increasingly violent methods used by the elites in Guatemala, El Salvador, Honduras, Nicaragua, and Panama to suffocate worker protests and rebellions. During the last half of the twentieth century, the political elite in these nations have used their nation's police force to kidnap, torture, and murder in order to terrorize the nation's poor into submission. These "dirty wars" killed hundreds of thousands of civilians between the conclusion of World War II and the end of the cold war in 1991. A variety of factors help us understand why governments behaved so savagely:

- Normal market fluctuations as had occurred for more than a century
- Prolonged longevity resulting in rapidly expanding populations of poor
- The Lend-Lease program during World War II, which placed advanced weapons in the hands of ruthless dictators such as Somoza (Nicaragua) and Ubico (Guatemala)
- The specter of the cold war, so often invoked by leaders to justify injustice
- Central Intelligence Agency operations in the region, aimed at undermining even democratically elected heads of state
- Narcotics trafficking and money laundering

Scholars have frequently sought to blame outside factors for the unrest that has plagued Central America in recent decades. Some authors, for example, blame the United States for Panama's rash of military dictators in recent decades. Other scholars have blamed Soviet and Cuban aggression for problems in 1970s- and 1980s-Nicaragua and El Salvador. Both of these arguments offer compelling explanations for the repression and civil war that has plagued Central America; they also provide an easily packaged and understood explanation and assignment of guilt. Such explanations, however, frequently overlook the people who live in these countries. In each of the seven nations, a very tiny elite (at times less than 1 percent of the population) goes to great lengths to protect their privileged status, while a huge majority of the nation's peoples (more than 95 percent) struggle desperately to eke out an existence.

This dialectic between rich and poor, powerful and subservient, lies at the core of recent violence in Central America. When compounded by the external realities outlined previously, this relationship between governor and governed has grown violent and bloody.

EL SALVADOR

Throughout the last half of the remainder of the twentieth century, the oligarchy and the military worked in tandem to control

El Salvador's political system and its economy; however, these ambitions became increasingly difficult to achieve with the passage of time. Thanks in part to inoculations and other medical advances, El Salvador's population grew faster than its food supply, placing a premium on land ownership and straining relations between land owners and peasants. The proportion of landless peasants increased from 11.8 percent in 1950 to more than 40 percent in the 1970s. Landlessness left the vast majority of El Salvador's people perilously vulnerable to illness and starvation; in the 1960s and 1970s, Salvadorans had the lowest per capita calorie intake of any Central American nation.

In a rather curious way, the problems of population growth and land ownership spilled over into foreign policy in April 1969. Soccer teams from El Salvador and Honduras had played a series of hard-fought games in the qualifying round of the 1969 World Cup. Both countries belonged to the Central American Common Market (CACM), created in 1961 to foster economic growth in the region. Honduras's economy hinged on the sale of bananas, and its industrial development lagged far behind that of El Salvador. Many Hondurans deeply resented their nation's relative underdevelopment and believed that their banana crop was being used by the CACM to subsidize Salvadoran industry. Hondurans also deeply resented the presence of 300,000 Salvadoran refugees who had fled El Salvador's land crush and settled illegally across the border in Honduras.

In April 1969, Honduras ordered many of these refugees back to El Salvador, and eventually 80,000 were expelled. In July 1969, the Salvadoran military responded by invading Honduras and destroying most of its air force on the ground. Cumulatively, these exchanges between Honduras and El Salvador became known as the Soccer War. The Soccer War was popular among many Salvadorans, but it cost the nation dearly. El Salvador lost access to the Honduran market for the next decade—a small market, but one that had been an important consumer of Salvadoran goods. More significantly, the return of tens of thousands of Salvadorans from Honduras placed much additional pressure on the nation's swollen population of landless rural poor.

Beyond these problems in the Salvadoran countryside, the nation's urban poor fared little better. Inflation was rampant, exceeding 60 percent in the 1970s, and unemployment and underemployment were widespread. To control the nation under these circumstances,

El Salvador's military resorted to increasingly blatant acts of violence and political chicanery. In 1972, for example, a civilian named Napoleon Duarte won the presidential election by more than 60,000 votes. The election of a civilian threatened to upset the precarious balance of power that the military and the wealthy had established, so the military decided to intervene and change the results of the election. The armed forces nullified the election and declared that a military officer, Colonel Armando Molina, had in reality won the election by 100,000 votes. Napoleon Duarte, the candidate who had won the election, was arrested, tortured, and forced into exile.

In 1977, in another blatantly fraudulent election, the military anointed General Carlos Humberto Romero president of the republic. As new opposition groups sprung up and guerilla activities increasingly challenged the military's right to govern, General Romero took the use of violence as a political option to a new level. Shortly after taking office, Romero issued the Law for the Defense and Guarantee of Public Order in November 1977, removing nearly all restrictions of armed violence against civilians and effectively declaring "open season" for soldiers to shoot anyone associated with (or presumed to associate with) leftists. On Romero's watch, death squad activity accelerated, as did the number of "disappearances" among El Salvador's poor.

In the months after the issuance of Romero's Public Order law, the political situation in El Salvador deteriorated rapidly. On the left, various revolutionary organizations banded together despite ideological differences to challenge the government. Guerilla groups, Communists, and other activists joined forces under umbrella organizations such as the *Frente de Acción Popular Unida* (Front for United Popular Action—FAPU) to rob banks, seize radio and television stations, take hostages, and assassinate political opponents. On the right, the military had established the *Organización Democrática Nacionalista* (Democratic Nationalist Organization—ORDEN) in the 1960s, and by the late 1970s, ORDEN had grown into a paramilitary vigilante group with nearly 80,000 members, including many prominent military officers. In 1977, an even more violently conservative group emerged from the officers' corps, a right-wing terrorist organization known as the White Warrior's Union, established by Roberto D'Aubuisson. In 1982, D'Aubuisson established the political party, *Alianza Republicana Nacionalista* (Nationalist Republican Alliance—ARENA), to give political legitimacy to the far right.

Archbishop Romero

As civil unrest and violence expanded in the late 1970s, President Romero and his allies in ORDEN and other right-wing groups encountered resistance from an unexpected source: the Catholic Church. Father Oscar Romero became Archbishop of El Salvador in 1977, and soon found himself entangled in the struggle between El Salvador's mighty and its poor. Initially very conservative, Archbishop Romero gradually evolved into a voice for the poor. He took umbrage with the extreme violence the government used to terrorize its political opponents, including the murder of various priests. During his tenure as Archbishop (1977–1980), Father Romero became increasingly strident and vocal in his denouncements of the military's abuses. He called the government and the military to repentance, denounced the United States for providing weapons to the Salvadoran military, and called on his followers to remain vigilant in the cause of justice.

Archbishop Romero became the beloved spokesman for poor Salvadorans everywhere, and this popularity placed him increasingly at odds with the military. This clash reached a crescendo in the early months of 1980, and on March 23, he publicly demanded that soldiers stop the repression. The next day, a military gunmen acting on orders from Roberto D'Aubuisson shot and killed the archbishop with a high-powered rifle while he celebrated mass in the chapel of the San Salvador's Divine Providence cancer hospital.

Archbishop Romero's murder sent a chilling message to the military's enemies: if the military and its death squads would kill the archbishop, they would kill anyone in the country who might dare to challenge them. Archbishop Romero's tragic death sparked a decade-long civil war that pitted the violent right-wing military apparatus and its political party, ARENA, against leftists who organized themselves anew under one name, the *Frente Farabundo Martí de Liberación Nacional* (Farabundo Martí National Liberation front—FMLN), invoking the Communist guerilla leader murdered by government forces in 1932.

In 1988, with the economy in ruins and civil war raging, the violent right-wing ARENA party gained control of the nation's parliament. The next year, ARENA expanded its reach when its candidate, Alfredo Cristiani, became president. Cristiani, one of D'Aubuisson's protégés, initially expressed a willingness to negotiate peace talks with FMLN guerillas but insisted they disarm completely before any cease-fire and negotiations. The guerillas refused, and both sides immediately returned to the battlefield. On November 1, 1989, international attention once again focused on the escalating violence, as Salvadoran troops stormed the University of Central America campus in San Salvador and executed six Jesuit priests, their housekeeper, and her 16-year-old daughter.

The longevity of the FMLN and its ability to strike targets all over the country brought increased international attention to El Salvador's civil war. No one was winning, thousands of people were dying, and the nation's economy was being devastated. Industry in El Salvador was operating at barely 40 percent of capacity, and labor unrest fed the continuation of the civil war. Human rights observers reported that 355 civilians were killed between July and November of 1990, all but 10 at the hands of the military. In 1991, ongoing violence brought additional international pressure to bear on the Salvadoran government, and in March of that year the country held legislative and municipal elections. FMLN boycotted the election and announced that no election would occur in the regions they controlled, but they offered an olive branch by announcing that they would not interfere in elections held elsewhere in the country. The March 1991 election was marred by fraud and intimidation, but it also bore some remarkable fruit: ARENA failed to win a majority in the legislature, and leftist opposition candidates won 20 percent of the vote. In May, ARENA leaders helped get Rubén Zamora, a prominent leftist leader, elected as one of the vice presidents of the legislative assembly.

Observers tend to speak of El Salvador's civil war as an event that began in 1980 and ended with the signing of the peace accord in January 1992. Certainly elections in the early 1990s signaled a new era of coexistence and brought an end to the chronic, acute violence that had torn the nation asunder. Even a cursory look at El Salvador in the mid-1990s, however, suggests that the conflict may be on "hold' rather than being over. Despite the increasingly representative nature of El Salvador's elections since the peace agreement was signed, the ARENA party has controlled the presidency. Most recently, on March 21, 2004, ARENA candidate Elías Antonio Saca González defeated FMLN candidate Schafik Jorge Handal, winning 58 percent of the vote to 35 percent for Handal, with an unprecedented 67 percent voter turnout. Until March 2003, ARENA had also controlled the legislative assembly; in the March 2003 legislative elections, the FMLN won 31 seats in the 84-seat legislative assembly and ARENA won 29 seats.

Beyond these initial steps toward representative government, a number of right-wing groups emerged in the mid-1990s, leveling death threats against priests, political enemies, and officers of the FMLN. In June 1996, for example, a group calling itself *Fuerza Nacionalista Mayor Roberto D'Aubuisson* (Nationalist Force Roberto D'Aubuisson—FURODA) issued public death threats to 15 prominent Salvadorans while referring to them as *gusanos* (worms). The FURODA hit list included clergy, FMLN leaders, and politicians. Other right-wing terrorist groups that emerged during this period include the *Sombra Negra* (Black Shadow), the *Organización Maximiliano Hernández Martínez contra el Críimen* (Organization Maximiliano Hernández Martínez Against Crime), and a handful of others. The Sombra Negra group fancies itself a "social clean-up squad," and by 1994 had murdered 17 people. In May 1995, Sombra Negra issued death threats against six Salvadoran judges.

The 1992 Chapultapec Peace Accord formally ended a civil war (1980-1991) that had pitted conservative and liberal activists against one another in pitched battles that claimed more than 70,000 lives. The years that followed illustrated some of the achievements and limitations of the peace process. El Salvador's political system began to gradually change and become more inclusive, ultimately resulting in a legislative assembly nearly evenly divided between ARENA and FMLN members. This must be considered the first step. ARENA has dominated the nation's presidency since well before the peace accord, and right-wing activists continue to form death squads and threaten their opponents with death. The spirit of the Chapultapec accord will be fully realized when El Salvador has a democratically-elected president and when no death squads menace Salvadoran society.

GUATEMALA

In 1950, then president Juan José Arévalo honored his own campaign pledge against reelection; he did not run again and left office peacefully. The 1950 election differed from Guatemala's previous elections due, in large part, to Arévalo's reforms. During Arévalo's tenure, literate women gained the right to vote, and political parties (Communists excluded) were permitted to organize themselves and to participate freely in the nation's elections. Guatemala was moving gradually toward a representative government that would more accurately reflect the wishes of the people instead of foreign companies.

As the 1950 election approached, Arévalo's Secretary of Defense, Jacobo Arbenz Guzmán, campaigned for the presidency on a platform of agrarian reform. On election day he carried the moment, winning 60 percent of the vote. On assuming office, he undertook implementing the reforms he had promised during the campaign. He built new roads and ports to enable Guatemala to function independently of United Fruit Company (UFCO), which had monopolized the nation's transportation system for many years.

Beyond his transportation initiatives, Arbenz made good his campaign promise to effect agrarian reform. As was the case elsewhere in Central America, the inequalities of land distribution in Guatemala stagger the imagination. Approximately 2 percent of the population controlled 72 percent of the nation's arable land. Conversely, 88 percent of the population controlled only 14 percent of the nation's farm land, leaving the vast majority of the population dependent on a small landed minority. Of all privately held lands, only 12 percent was under cultivation. The large majority of Guatemala's farmlands were owned by a small landed elite and laying fallow.

Decree 900

On June 17, 1952, Arbenz's administration enacted Decree 900, the Agrarian Reform Law of 1952. As stated in the preamble to the law, Decree 900 had as its purpose, "to liquidate feudal property in the countryside and the relations of production that it originates in order to develop the form of exploitation and capitalist methods of production in agriculture and to prepare the way for the industrialization of Guatemala." This decree mandated that all unused lands larger than 223 acres be expropriated, with the previous owner receiving government bonds equal to the state tax value of the land. Over the course of the reform (1952–1954), the Arbenz regime paid out $8,345,545 in government bonds for these expropriated lands.

This reform hit UFCO particularly hard. UFCO controlled 550,000 acres of land, 85 percent of which lay fallow. Of their land, approximately 400,000 acres were expropriated and distributed to 50,000 peasants. During the twos of agrarian reform, Decree 900 redistributed 1,491,785 acres of land to approximately 100,000 Guatemalan families.

UFCO officials were infuriated by the loss of their land and by the price offered as compensation. For years UFCO and other companies operating in Latin America grossly understated the value of their operations to avoid paying high taxes, sometimes stating a value one-tenth the actual book value. Caught in their own trap, UFCO and U.S. government officials contended that Guatemala had been infiltrated by Communist subversives who used agrarian reform to establish a beachhead in the Americas.

Two powerful UFCO lawyers now held influential positions within the U.S. government, and they used their influence to fan the flames of suspicion toward Guatemala. John Foster Dulles, U.S. Secretary of State, used his office as a forum before the United Nations to condemn the "Communist infiltration" in Guatemala. Dulles's brother, Alan Dulles, was Director of the Central Intelligence Agency (CIA) and shared his brother's desire to reverse the agrarian reforms in Guatemala. With the guidance of the Dulles brothers, the United States government made plans to overthrow the Arbenz regime, reverse the reforms, and return UFCO lands. The plan that was agreed upon was OPERATION PBSUCCESS.

In May 1954, a shipment of weapons from Czechoslovakia arrived in Guatemala, offering the United States the moment they had waited for. Communist-bloc weapons had been banned in Guatemala, and their arrival served as a pretext to accuse Arbenz of being a Communist, which in turn provided the pretext necessary for the military overthrow of Arbenz.

The United States chose a junior officer, Carlos Castillo Armas, as the appropriate successor to Arbenz. In June 1954, Castillo Armas entered Guatemala from Honduras and launched his assault on the Arbenz regime. With support from the CIA and the U.S. State Department, Arbenz and his men advanced on the capital city, where the Guatemalan police had decided not to intervene in behalf of Arbenz. The chaos in the countryside provoked by the reforms had alienated army officers, who resented Arbenz for not adequately moving to control the restless rural poor.

With the CIA and the U.S. State Department on Castillo Armas' side, and with the army unwilling to take up arms in Arbenz's defense, Arbenz was forced to resign and go into exile. Castillo Armas immediately revoked Decree 900 and returned power and property to the landed elite and their foreign *patrones.* Beyond this,

Castillo Armas used the nation's armed forces to terrorize anyone who had participated in the reform. Some scholars estimate that Castillo Armas executed 8,000 people for their affiliation with the Arbenz reforms.

The Castillo Armas-led counterrevolution went well beyond merely reversing Decree 900. Since 1954, the average size of peasant holdings has decreased, and the amount of land used for commercial farming has increased markedly. Although Castillo Armas himself was assassinated in 1957, his legacy continues to affect life in Guatemala. Since 1954, Guatemala's working poor has been violently repressed by death squads, gunmen hired by employers to eliminate troublesome employees.

Today in Guatemala the civil war continues in parts of the countryside. In the 1970s and 1980s, tens of thousands of peasants, largely Indian, were executed under the guise of "fighting communism." At the end of the twentieth century, Guatemala's military still remains in control of the countryside, and in the 1990s Guatemala frequently earned the dubious epitaph of Central America's worst violator of human rights. By the time the government and the guerrillas signed the peace accord in 1996, 160,000 people had been killed and 40,000 "disappeared"—93 percent at the hands of the Guatemalan security forces, according to "Guatemala: Memory of Silence," the report of the Historical Clarification Commission.

HONDURAS

In 1948, the aging military dictator, Tiburcio Carías, stepped down peacefully and turned over the presidency to his minister of defense, Juan Manuel Gálvez. Gálvez had been an attorney for American banana companies doing business in Honduras, but he proved not to be the American lackey his foes accused him of being. He modernized roads, established the Central Bank, and promoted coffee exports. As he prepared to leave office in 1954, banana workers went on strike. Given his ties to the banana companies, Gálvez did not dare to intervene with force. Without military repression, strikers achieved a series of goals, most notably the legalization of unions in Honduras.

The presidential election of 1954 pitted Carías (apparently well rested from his previous tenure as dictator) against liberal candidate Dr. Ramón Villeda Morales, a pediatrician who favored civil rights, land reform, the right of labor to organize, and revision of the government's onerous contract with the UFCO. In Honduras's first free election since 1932, Villeda won the election with 48 percent of the vote. Carías' friends in Congress, however, refused to acknowledge Villeda's victory. Gálvez's vice president, Julio Lozano Díaz, seized power and established another military dictatorship.

This game of musical chairs among military dictators continued in Honduras until 1957, when liberals gained an absolute majority in the Congress. Divisions within the officer corps of the military had ended when a group of younger officers stepped in and allowed liberals to participate and to assume the offices they had fairly won. In November 1957, the liberal-dominated Constituent Assembly elected Villeda president of the republic. The younger officers did not intervene, and Honduras thus ended 24 years of military dictatorships.

The success of Fidel Castro in the Cuban revolution spooked conservative military officers all over Latin America, including Honduras. Villeda's enemies accused him of being linked to Moscow and Communist forces in Cuba, and in October 1963, the military removed Villeda from office. Over the next two decades Honduras had a series of military dictators who controlled the federal government. By 1975, circumstances had become so convoluted that one military dictator, Commander Oswaldo López Arellano, was overthrown in a military coup and replaced by another military-dominated regime, which was, in turn, toppled in 1978 by yet another military coup.

The "Pentagon Republic"

The Sandinista revolution in Nicaragua further complicated the political situation in Honduras. Anastasio Somoza had been a close friend and supporter of Honduras for many years, and now a hostile Communist regime lay just across the border. From Washington, President Carter pressured the Honduran military to hold open elections and return the country to constitutional rule. In the November 1981 election, liberal Roberto Suazo Córdoba won the presidency decisively and led his country back to the rule of law. Once again, however, circumstances made Honduran moderates look weak on communism; as Suazo took office, thousands of former Somoza National Guardsmen amassed on the Honduran side of the border and were in the early stages of a guerilla-style counterrevolutionary struggle against the Sandinistas. Meanwhile, 10,000 Miskito Indians immigrated to Honduras from Nicaragua's Caribbean Coast, adding to the squalid living circumstances in parts of remote Honduras.

Soon, thousands of U.S. military personnel joined Honduran military forces in policing Honduras while training the Contra fighting force. The presence of ex-Somoza guardsmen/Contras, coupled with the presence of thousands of American troops, militarized the Honduran state and placed extraordinary stress on the nation. President Suazo remained in power because he had a cadre of young officers who were loyal to him. In 1986, another liberal, José Azcona Hoyo, succeeded Suazo to the presidency, again with the support of some of the younger officers in the Honduran military, who felt keenly the anti-Americanism that had arisen as a result of the presence of so many U.S. troops in Honduras. The 1986 election and transition marked the first peaceful transfer of power between civilian presidents in 30 years.

In the mid-1980s, the massive American presence helped the nation's economy, which kept working-class protests to a minimum, which in turn kept the ardent conservatives placated. Had the economy not experienced any kind of relief, it is difficult to imagine the Honduran people tolerating what was happening on their soil, at least not willingly. The Americans built bridges and roads, constructed new military bases, and spent tens of millions of dollars in the Honduran economy. Sadly, this economic boom also deepened Honduras's fiscal reliance on the United States.

In 1990, yet another civilian, Rafael Callejas, became president. Callejas undertook an aggressive reform program aimed at reforming the nation's economy. He also took unprecedented steps to place the military under civilian control. Even when problems in the banana sector caused per capita income in Honduras to drop from $534 per year in 1990 to $205 in 1992, the military remained calm and did not intervene.

In 1998, Honduras elected its fifth civilian president since the constitutional reforms of 1981, Carlos Roberto Flores Facusse. As president, Flores completed the transition of the military by eliminating the post of commander in chief within the military, instead creating a civilian minister of defense position with authority over the military. Many of Honduras's hopes for reform went on hold in

October 1998 when Hurricane Mitch devastated Honduras. Mitch left 5,000 dead and 1.5 million homeless, causing approximately $2 billion in damage.

At the beginning of the twenty-first century, Honduras continues to deal with the economic repercussions of Hurricane Mitch. It is among the poorest nations in the Western Hemisphere and is more economically dependent on the United States than any other nation in Central America. Unemployment exceeds 20 percent, and the disparity in income distribution remains dangerously high. These social and economic factors provide fertile ground for military intervention, but thus far Honduras has clung successfully to the constitutional reforms of 1981. History suggests, however, that to endure economically difficult times, civilian leaders must take austere steps to stabilize the plight of the working poor. In the past, economically difficult times exacerbated by natural disaster have bred military intervention as the wealthy become nervous and seek armed solutions.

NICARAGUA

When U.S. military forces left Nicaragua for the last time in 1933, they left a hand-picked commander of the new National Guard who would govern Nicaragua in the absence of *Yanqui* troops. This new commander, Anastasio Somoza García, soon proved himself a tyrannical military dictator who governed Nicaragua with an iron fist. First indications of Somoza's ruthlessness occurred on February 21, 1934, after a special dinner Augusto César Sandino had attended with Nicaragua's elected president, Juan B. Sacasa. Sandino had carried on a years-long struggle against occupying American forces and, when the last of the Americans had withdrawn, Sacasa invited Sandino to the presidential palace in Managua to establish a cordial working relationship. Sacasa had personally guaranteed Sandino's safety, and yet, as the nationalist patriot left the palace, National Guard Commander Somoza arrested Sandino. The Guard then took Sandino to the airfield and executed him.

The Somoza Dynasty

After Sandino's murder, Somoza continued to openly defy President Sacasa. In 1936, Somoza ran for president, taking care to incorporate control of the National Guard into his duties as president-elect. From his election in 1936 to his assassination in 1956, Somoza used the presidency to enrich himself and his family while brutally suppressing any economic or political dissidence. A few brief years into his presidency, Somoza had consolidated control of Nicaragua's political system, its economy, and its military. A selfish, brutal dictator, Somoza controlled his nation's resources to an extent that exceeded any of his dictatorial peers in Central America. Certainly Guatemala's Ubico never approached this level of domination, and Somoza probably had more thorough control of his country than the oligarchy/military tandem in El Salvador.

When an assassin felled Anastasio Somoza García in 1956, his son Luis Somoza Debayle became Nicaragua's new president. Then, when Luis's health began to fail in 1967, his younger brother Anastasio Somoza Debayle (also known as "Tachito") got himself elected president. Two months later, Luis died of a heart attack and left his brother Anastasio the sole guardian of the dynasty. As the world would learn on December 23, 1972, the young Anastasio may have been the most corrupt, greedy Somoza of them all.

On December 23, a large earthquake destroyed 80 percent of Managua's business district, killing 10,000 persons and leaving 50,000 homeless. As massive quantities of emergency foreign aid flowed in, Somoza's National Guard looted while the dictator illegally appropriated tens of millions of dollars sent to Nicaragua to relieve suffering.

The earthquake and its aftermath galvanized opposition to Somoza, and opposition leaders became increasingly vocal and public in their demands for political pluralism. Calls for Somoza to step down reached a crescendo, and yet in 1974 Somoza once again declared himself the winner of a fixed election. The recurring, blatant election fraud coupled with Somoza's theft of emergency aid sparked overt opposition unlike any that had existed previously in Nicaragua. In the late 1950s, a group of about 20 students at Managua's *Universidad Nacional Autónoma de Nicaragua* (National Autonomous University of Nicaragua) established an underground student activist group to oppose the Somoza dictatorship. In 1961, three leaders of this movement—José Carlos Fonseca Amador, Silvio Mayorga, and Tomás Borge Martínez—formally organized the group into the *Frente Sandinista de Liberación Nacional* (Sandinista National Liberation Front—FSLN) and called themselves *Sandinistas*. Over the next several years, FSLN led a low-intensity guerilla movement against Somoza. Over the course of the 1960s, Fonseca, Mayorga, and Borge were incarcerated and forced into exile by the Somoza dictatorship, only to return and pick up the cause.

Somoza's blatantly criminal handling of the 1972 earthquake disaster profoundly affected the FSLN, which was gradually gaining support from peasants and workers. On December 27, 1974, members of the FSLN raided a private party in Managua and took 40 hostages, including relatives of Somoza and various members of the regime. During the next three days, the FSLN hostage takers made a series of demands: a $1 million ransom; a declaration read over the radio and printed in *La Prensa* newspaper; release of 14 FSLN members held in Somoza's prisons; and safe transport of the FSLN members and the hostage takers to Havana. Nicaragua's archbishop, Father Miguel Obando y Bravo, mediated negotiations, and on December 30, the government acquiesced to all the demands.

The hostage crisis of December 1974 proved supremely embarrassing to the Nicaraguan government, which responded with new waves of violent political repression in rural areas suspected of harboring pro-FSLN activists. Conversely, the hostage crisis greatly enhanced the prestige of the FSLN among thousands of Nicaraguans, who now saw terrorism as a means to successfully negotiate with the Somoza dictatorship. Moreover, one of the 14 FSLN prisoners released and flown to Cuba was Daniel Ortega Saavedra, who would return to Nicaragua and help lead the successful revolution against Somoza in the late 1970s.

The Sandinista Revolution

Through the mid-1970s, a series of events had alienated Nicaraguans from their government, most notably the Somoza family's illegal continuance in office and its blatant disregard for law, and human life, during the 1972 earthquake crisis. In January 1978, Pedro Joachim Chamorro, beloved publisher of *La Prensa* and ardent anti-Somoza activist, had just published a series of articles titled, "Crónicas del Vampiro" ("Vampire Chronicles"), denouncing the commercial blood-plasma operation through which Somoza sold the blood of his people to the United States. In response to these articles, Somoza's regime assassinated Chamorro on January 10, 1978, sparking mass demonstrations in Managua and throughout much of the country.

The Chamorro assassination stunned all Nicaraguans. He came from one of Nicaragua's oldest, wealthiest families. Many upper-class Nicaraguans could overlook Somoza's brutality with Indians and peasants, but this time he had killed one of their own class. Many Nicaraguans believed that if Pedro Joaquin Chamorro could be killed, no one was safe.

On August 22, 1978, the Sandinistas carried off their most brazen attack on the Somoza government. Twenty-five Sandinistas stormed the National palace, taking hostages including members of the Chamber of Deputies and approximately 2,000 public employees. Once again, after frantic negotiations by Somoza, the guerillas' demands—a huge ransom, release of 59 Sandinistas currently in jail, and safe flight for the guerillas and released hostages to Panama—were met.

On September 8, the Sandinistas launched simultaneous uprisings in five different cities, keeping the government on the defensive. Somoza responded by ordering his air force to bomb each city, after which his troops retook the towns one at a time. Somoza then ordered "Operation Clean-up," a house-to-house search-and-destroy mission that left 5,000 Nicaraguans dead. Each time Somoza responded with ruthless abandon, thousands more Nicaraguans joined the Sandinista revolution. Increasingly, many Nicaraguans came to view violent response as the only way to survive their government's whims.

After the September uprisings, both sides mobilized for the pitched civil war that was coming. Peasants stockpiled food for the Sandinista army, which had grown from a few hundred to thousands. The final showdown came the next year, in June 1979. That month the FSLN called for a general strike, and on June 8, the Sandinista army breached the perimeters of Managua. For a month the two sides fought a pitched battle in the streets of the capital, with Somoza retreating to his hastily constructed bunker. From the safety of his bunker, he ordered a massive air and artillery assault on the city without any regard for innocent civilians. The massive artillery campaign he unleashed seemed to destroy anything that had survived the 1972 earthquake.

On July 16, 1979, Somoza agreed to resign and go into exile. The next day he went to the airport and left Nicaragua forever. On July 18, the Sandinistas formally entered Managua as the victorious army. Their provisional government included the anti-Somoza businessman, Alfonso Robelo, and the moderate widow of Pedro Joaquin

Chamorro. This moderate governing body lasted only a short time, though, because soon after taking power the revolution turned markedly to the left, alienating its moderate supporters. Within a short period of time, Robelo and Chamorro would disavow themselves of the revolution and resign their government posts. Moderation was not going to a be a Sandinista strength.

By the end of 1979, the Sandinista government had expropriated (without compensation) nearly 20 percent of the nation's arable land, most of which had belonged to the Somoza family and its associates. Conservatives inside and outside Managua grew increasingly alarmed with Nicaragua's strident new government. In 1980, Ronald Reagan became President of the United States and declared war on the Sandinistas, vowing to prevent the Soviets from establishing a Communist beachhead in Central America.

In 1983, the Reagan administration's "secret war" against the Sandinistas went into high gear. In Honduras, American Ambassador to Honduras, John Negroponte, helped launch a ragtag army of mercenaries, Somoza soldiers-in-exile, and Honduran troops into a fighting force the world would know as the *Contras* (meaning counter-revolutionaries) whom Reagan would liken to the Founding Fathers of the United States. Over the next several years, civil war pitted the Contras against the Sandinistas in a civil war that bounced back-and-forth across borders and that sowed much destruction and death.

Despite the expenditure of tens of millions of dollars in support of the Contra force, by the mid-1980s the Sandinistas could legitimately point to some successes. Literacy rates, life expectancy, and other social indicators seemed to be inching upward, suggesting that the Sandinistas were making inroads in important areas of society. During the war they had promised to hold open and fair elections, and in 1984 they honored their promise and conducted a presidential election that included many international observers. The Sandinistas received 67 percent of the vote, and Daniel Ortega became the elected president of Nicaragua. By 1986, the Sandinistas had achieved a surprising "strategic victory" over the Contras, figuring out military tactics that enabled them to defend Nicaragua's coffee harvests, for example, from Contra terrorist strikes intended to devastate the Nicaraguan economy.

Despite these advances, the government of Nicaragua faced some difficult realities. The strident Marxism of the revolution's leaders fractured the broad-based support the Sandinistas had briefly enjoyed, costing them the support of moderates, including wealthy industrialists who had initially supported their war against Somoza. Equally significant, the Nicaraguan economy was a disaster. Every year between 1984 and 1990, Nicaragua's gross domestic product declined. Unable to secure foreign loans, the government printed more money, resulting in runaway inflation that exceeded 14,000 percent in 1988. This rampant inflation cost the Sandinistas the support of much of Nicaragua's poor and middle classes, groups who bore the brunt of this financial crisis. When the Ortega government took steps toward austerity to correct the inflation, Hurricane Joan struck and caused extensive damage to Nicaragua's agriculture. Throughout the entire period, they also spent large sums of money fighting the Contras, and the U.S. embargo prevented them from getting access to goods and services that might have saved them.

Nicaragua's moderate wealthy and its workers were not the only elements of Nicaraguan society alienated by the Sandinistas. It soon became apparent that the Sandinista leadership was naïve regarding Native Americans living in Nicaragua. Sandinista writings displayed an ethnocentrism that seemed not to acknowledge the indigenous struggle for equality, depicting Indians as passive characters in history, unjustly subjugated by White Europeans. Marxist dogma (naïve as it is regarding indigenous peoples) suggested simply that indigenous peoples, like all others, ought to be assimilated into society as quickly as possible. The results were stunning. By late 1981, Nicaragua's entire East Coast had become militarized, and 10,000 Miskito had been forced out of their homes by the Sandinistas and placed in relocation camps; 15,000 Miskitos had escaped across the border into Honduras, where many joined the Contra movement.

Nicaragua's 1990 Election

By most standards, Nicaraguans were poorer in 1990 than they had been in 1970. The Sandinistas had made significant progress in a number of areas involving social issues, but the election of 1990 suggests that for most Nicaraguans, the social progress of the 1980s did not outweigh the financial and other hardships of the Sandinista years. As the February 25, 1990, election approached, most observers believed the FSLN would carry the day despite the nation's many hardships. Yet, in a stunning upset, opposition candidate

Violetta Chamorro defeated Daniel Ortega, winning 54 percent of votes cast compared to Ortega's 44 percent. Nicaraguans had repudiated the Sandinista revolution at the ballot box.

Equally surprising was the way in which the Sandinistas responded to victory. Although they had the military capability to annul the election and simply declare themselves the winners, they did not do so. Daniel Ortega and other Sandinista leaders seemed to have a difficult time accepting defeat, but they nonetheless peacefully relinquished control they had fought long and hard to obtain.

The 1990 election did not end Nicaragua's many challenges. At the beginning of the twenty-first century, land distribution in Nicaragua continues to be among the worst of any nation in the world. The nation is saddled with huge foreign debts, unemployment is rampant, and more than 50 percent of the population lives below poverty level. The nation's political situation has not entirely stabilized; the president who succeeded Violetta Chamorro, Arnoldo Aleman, is now in a jail in Managua for having pilfered tens of millions of dollars from federal coffers. Meanwhile, former president Daniel Ortega has become the nation's celebrated perpetual candidate for the presidency. Ortega has run for president each election year since 1989 and has lost each time.

NOTE

1. Panamanians use the term *paquetazo* (stuffing the ballot box) to describe election fraud there. In one infamous case of *paquetazo*, the president's hand-picked successor in the 1936 elections won more votes in the rural province of Veraguas than was possible. The number of votes in some areas exceeded the number of voters. The elite accomplished this by crating fictitious names and by voting in behalf of persons long since deceased. In Panama, even the dead vote—sometimes more than once.

7

The Cold War II: Belize, Costa Rica, and Panama

In the years after World War II, Central American nations found themselves being transformed into cold war battlefields. U.S. officials had provided huge amounts of cash and considerable military hardware to its Central American allies, several of whom were ruthless military dictators. Conversely, as the cold war progressed, weapons and cash from the Soviet Union made their way to Central America. Though much smaller in size, this Soviet support helped ensure that those opposed to U.S.-backed dictators would have a means of fighting back against political repression. In El Salvador, Guatemala, and Nicaragua the flow of foreign arms and support underwrote violent civil wars that killed hundreds of thousands of people.

The nations of Belize, Costa Rica, and Panama provided an alternative view of Central America during the cold war. These three nations did not experience protracted civil wars with tens of thousands of deaths and vast economic destruction, but they experienced profound changes caused by the ongoing crisis. As civil wars raged elsewhere, Belize, Costa Rica, and Panama each absorbed thousands of political refugees who had fled the bloodshed of their homelands. Meanwhile, although Costa Rica remained neutral and largely aloof from the cold war (excepting its 1948 crisis), Belize and

Panama experienced the brunt of the cold war in other ways. After its independence in the early 1980s, Belize fell under considerable condemnation by allying itself more closely with the United States. And, in December 1989, Panamanians learned firsthand that the United States still considered military invasion an option when its diplomatic efforts failed to produce the desired results.

BELIZE

During and immediately after World War II, Belize suffered from two serious problems: declining supplies of unharvested timber and a flood of workers who went elsewhere for work—to Panama to work on the Canal, to England to work in the timber industry, and so forth. For those who remained in Belize, things took a marked turn for the worse in December 1949, when the British devalued the Belizean dollar, immediately lowering the wages and purchasing power of Belize's workers.

On September 29, 1950, protestors against the British system formed the People's United Party (PUP), which had as its stated objective, "to gain for the people of this country political independence and economic independence." In the 1930s, Antonio Soberanis (nationalist and labor organizer) had been a pioneer in articulating public opposition to the British imperial system, and now the PUP expanded on his message. The PUP's platform was stridently nationalist and demanded the attention of British officials. Under the leadership of Leigh Richardson, George Price, and Philip Goldson, the PUP proclaimed that the hardships and destitution experienced by residents of Belize were due largely to colonial exploitation, which sent national wealth abroad while impoverishing the people and leaving them to live in squalor.

In 1951, the PUP forged a close alliance with the General Workers Union (GWU), and by the end of the year, the two organizations had many of the same leaders. Together, these two working-class organizations had to deal with the British and with members of the middle class, who favored preserving the British colonial system. The middle class argued that the nation needed to develop before it gained its independence, a point bitterly contested by the PUP and GWU membership.

In the end, workers carried the day. In 1954, the people of Belize gained the right of universal suffrage. In 1960, the United Nations passed a resolution calling for the independence of all persons still under colonial rule. The next year, Great Britain granted Belize self-rule, with the promise of constitutional independence in the near future. In 1973, the nation's name was changed from British Honduras to Belize, and then on September 21, 1981, Belize gained full constitutional independence from Great Britain. Belize's first prime minister was the venerable leader of the PUP, George Price. After the PUP split in the late 1950s, George Price emerged as the clear leader of the nationalist, pro-independence movement. When others waffled, Price favored full independence and the establishment of a sovereign nation of Belize. He also favored close relations with the other Central American countries, something opposed by his political enemies who feared the "Latinization" of Belize. By all accounts, Price was a leader with a revolutionary perspective who clearly grasped—and articulated—the necessity of sovereign independence, regional identity, and the strength of working together with the other Central American countries. He is the father of the nation of Belize.

As the nation moved toward independence, it experienced a series of profound changes that helped shape the new state. First, between 1971 and 1984, the nation experienced agrarian reform as the government distributed more than 500,000 acres to the working class. During this period, agriculture replaced the timber industry as Belize's principal export; timber exports declined from 80 percent in the 1950s to 1.9 percent in 1981.Also, the nation's population has doubled in the past three decades, in part because of the influx of thousands of persons fleeing civil wars elsewhere in the region.

COSTA RICA

In 1948, Costa Rica experienced the most profound political unrest in its history. Workers had suffered unemployment and declining wages over the course of the 1930s, and many (banana workers, for example) had begun organizing themselves to protest their circumstances. Amidst these stressful conditions, Rafael Angel Calderón Guardia ran for president in 1940 on the moderate National Republican Party ticket.

To expand his base of popular support during the election, Calderón Guardia had aligned himself with Costa Rica's *Vanguardia Popular* (Popular Vanguard), a small militant group that emerged in 1943 when the Communist Party disbanded. Calderón Guardia's courting of the left alarmed the nation's more conservative elite, and it also alarmed the administrations in Nicaragua, El Salvador, and elsewhere. Many Costa Ricans considered him a Communist.

During his term Calderón Guardia initiated a series of sweeping reforms aimed at relieving the suffering of the nation's poor. He founded the *Universidad de Costa Rica* in 1940; created Costa Rica's social security program, which still exists today; and took steps to guarantee the basic rights of all Costa Ricans. He also enacted a minimum wage law and took steps to protect workers' rights.

Calderón Guardia was succeeded by Teodoro Picado Michalski, who served as president from 1944 to 1948. Many considered Picado a Calderón Guardia puppet, keeping the proverbial presidential seat warm until Calderón Guardia was constitutionally eligible to run again for president in 1948. However, a number of significant things occurred during Picado's administration, not the least of which was the alliance he forged with Manuel Mora Valverde, organizer of the Communist Party and now the leader of the *Vanguardia*.

During Picado's term, conservative San José publisher Otilio Ulate Blanco formed a vehemently anti-Communist political party, the *Partido Union Nacional* (National Union Party—PUN), to challenge the Calderón Guardia faction in 1948. Meanwhile, José Figueres Ferrer established the *Partido Democrático Social* (Social Democratic Party). Figueres's new party was moderately leftist and progressive, but anti-Communist. Both new parties were suspicious of Communists, both felt keenly that Picado had given Communists a voice in his regime, and both intended to rid Costa Rica's government of Communism.

As the election approached, Calderón Guardia had a strong hold on the nation's electoral machinery, but widespread fear of a dictatorship and of communism pushed the election in favor of Ulate. On election day, when it became apparent that Ulate had won, the Calderón-controlled congress annulled the election and on March 1, 1948 declared Calderón the winner. Calderón supporters then had Ulate arrested and incarcerated.

At this critical juncture in Costa Rican history, Figueres performed heroically. He denounced the government and carried out small guerilla-like strikes in the region of the capital. Aided by financial and military assistance from Washington and from Arévalo in Guatemala, Figueres organized an April 11 assault on San Isidro del General (south of San José) and the next day personally led an occupying expedition to take the nation's most important religious center, Cartago (also south of San José). Meanwhile, a supporting group known as the Caribbean Legion (an assortment of anti-Communist fighters from the region) took the critical Atlantic port of Limón, effectively cutting off the railroad. Figueres's forces then immediately surrounded the capital city, cutting off transportation routes.

On April 13, most fighting stopped and negotiations began in earnest. The only remaining skirmishes taking place were attacks by Communist-led workers from the nation's banana industry, who fought valiantly for Calderón until April 19. At this point, Calderón Guardia and Picado went into exile in Mexico, and on April 24, Figueres's army marched triumphantly into San José. The victors selected Santos León Herrera to serve as interim chief of state while Figueres's PLN moved to restore order to the republic. The 1948 Costa Rican revolution, a 44-day civil war, claimed 2,000 lives and seriously disrupted a nation known for its peaceful way of life.

On May 8, 1948, José Figueres became chief of state of a "Second Republic" junta. At this point in his distinguished life as a public servant, Figueres had little popular support. He drafted a new constitution, which the Constituent Assembly rejected, and his candidates for the Constituent Assembly were roundly defeated in the December 1948 legislative election. Ulate's PUN won 33 seats, various allied parties won 8 seats, and Figueres's party won 4 seats. Conservatives were still leery of his moderately liberal views. In 1953, the nation would elect him president by a wide margin, but Costa Ricans did not yet know exactly what to make of Figueres.

Despite the setbacks he experienced in the months after the revolution, Figueres set in motion a series of pivotal changes that would become critical components of the modern Costa Rican state:

- Outlawed the Communist Party
- Abolished the army
- Promoted the development of the nation's energy resources

The Constituent Assembly rejected the constitution Figueres had crafted, which contained these changes (they also rejected his notion of a "Second Republic"), but it enacted a new constitution of its own that contained many of Figueres's most progressive ideas. Going beyond what he had proposed, the assembly's new constitution provided for a Supreme Electoral Tribunal, an independent judiciary, and provided equal rights for women. Figueres may have been a bit ahead of his time, but the nation's legislators and its people surely embraced many of his most important ideas almost immediately.

Once elected in his own right in 1953, Figueres, known to his countrymen as *"Don Pepe,"* proceeded forward quickly with his reforms. He renegotiated the nation's contracts with United Fruit Company, raised taxes in an effort to achieve fiscal solvency, and launched a series of public works projects, which had the effect of lowering unemployment. Figueres completed his term in 1958, having made significant social progress, despite his many critics who accused him of graft, leading the nation toward communism, and demagoguery. Nevertheless, as president, Figueres enacted various moderate social and economic reforms that contributed significantly to the shape of modern Costa Rica. Like Guardia in the 1870s, Figueres succeeded in striking a balance between liberals and conservatives. He provided for workers' needs while promoting industry, without scaring off either side.

Since Figueres left office, Costa Rica has been a model of democratic stability. The PLN has controlled the assembly since the 1950s, resulting in a series progressive legislation that has made Costa Rica the modern example of how to blend socialist and capitalist institutions under one constitution. During this same period, however, opposition parties have dominated the presidency. The PLN did not win a presidential election until Figueres was reelected in 1970.

In the last decades of the twentieth century, Costa Rica struggled through a prolonged fiscal crisis that included a huge foreign debt, weak currency, low prices for coffee and bananas, and ongoing social programs that continue to require a large amount of money. With civil wars in other parts of Central America, Costa Rica absorbed large numbers of political refugees, which placed additional burden on Costa Rica's already-taxed economy.

In the late 1980s and 1990s, though, a significant transition began in the nation's economy. Until the 1990s, agricultural and pastoral goods had been the staple of the economy, with tourism and foreign retirees who settled in Costa Rica contributing significantly. In the 1990s, manufacturing and industry replaced agriculture as the largest single contributor to Costa Rica's gross domestic product (GDP). Intel, Abbot Laboratories, Proctor and Gamble, and Baxter

Healthcare constitute a few of the most visible companies to locate in Costa Rica, drawn to the nation by its climate, its educated work force, and its political stability.

PANAMA

Throughout the first decades of the twentieth century, life in Panama had been dominated by a massive American military presence (tens of thousands of soldiers and support staff), nationalists who abhorred the occupying army, and successive Panamanian presidents who tried to exploit the American presence while placating the nationalists. This political conflict of interests became most apparent in December 1947, when tens of thousands of Panamanians from all walks of life went to the streets to protest President Jiménez's effort to make concessions to the United States that most Panamanians opposed.

Shortly after the Panamanian government established the *Universidad de Panamá* in 1935, Panamanians who studied at the university returned to their home communities to work and live, and they carried with them the nationalist ardor they had learned during their university educations in the capital city. Therefore in 1957, when students organized to commemorate the successful rejection of the treaty, demonstrations occurred all over the country. Schoolchildren in faraway provinces heard how their government had turned its guns and bayonets on Panamanian students, and a new generation of youth learned about *Yanqui* imperialism and oligarchic duplicity.

The 1957 commemoration of the Filós-Hines conflict resounded with students and activists throughout the nation. Student leaders, most notably from the *Unión de Estudiantes Universitarios* (Union of University Students), launched "Operation Sovereignty," including the first *siembra* (planting) movement, firmly planting Panamanian flags inside the Canal Zone to express their anger with U.S. imperialism and its effects in Panama. This was a particularly dangerous plan because American soldiers staffed the length of the high fence separating Panama City from the Canal Zone, and Panamanians were strictly prohibited from setting foot on the wrong side of the fence. Waiting patiently until U.S. troops guarding the entrance went on their coffee break, students dressed in neckties and suit coats entered the Canal Zone and planted 75 Panamanian flags inside the Canal Zone.

In October 1958, labor and student leaders continued their protests. In a large "Hunger and Desperation" march, thousands of protestors marched from Colón to Panama City to protest low wages, high rent, and general working conditions in the Canal Zone and throughout the republic. The next month, student organizers launched another protest. Beginning at 9:00 A.M. on November 3, 1959, student protestors marched toward the Canal Zone to raise dozens of Panamanian flags in the Canal Zone in an action known as *La Siembra de la Bandera* (the planting of the flag). In the resulting clash, more than 70 Panamanians were injured, and calm was restored only when Panama's National Guard declared martial law and occupied the terminal cities of Colón and Panamá.

In response to the "Flag Riots," U.S. President Dwight D. Eisenhower sent an emissary to Panama to consider ways that relations between the two nations might be improved. The result, "Operation Friendship," made some cursory economic gestures aimed at eliminating points of irritation between the two countries. During this same period, the Panamanian government and U.S. officials jointly announced that the United States would build a bridge across the canal at the edge of Panama City. This bridge, the Bridge of the Americas, replaced the ferry system that had served for decades, transporting persons and vehicles across the waterway from Panama's interior to the capital city.

Then in September, President Eisenhower issued an executive order that would become the focus of tremendous scrutiny and debate over the next few years. He ordered U.S. officials in Panama to fly the Panamanian flag alongside the U.S. flag at the U.S. embassy and at Shaler's Triangle (an important intersection in Panama City). Conservative Americans believed Eisenhower had yielded to Communist pressure; in reality, he grasped the precarious nature of U.S. relations with Panama. This was the right thing to do—something that the United States demands when foreign companies operate on U.S. soil—and obedience to the order would have saved considerable heartache and tragedy.

Despite this presidential order, though, Panama's flag did not fly in the Zone. In January 1963, President John F. Kennedy expanded on Eisenhower's order, instructing Canal Zone Governor Robert Fleming to fly Panama's flag at all nonmilitary sites in the Canal Zone where the Stars and Stripes flew. Fleming and other Americans living in the Canal Zone deeply resented Eisenhower and Kennedy for giving the

Panamanian flag prominence, and Fleming simply disregarded both orders: he acted as if the orders had not been issued. One month after Kennedy's murder in Dallas, Fleming issued orders restricting the implementation of Kennedy's decree. Rather than flying the flags of both countries as mandated by Kennedy, Fleming ordered that neither flag be flown at those areas designated in the Executive Order.

On January 7, 1964, American students in the Canal Zone disregarded Fleming's instructions by raising the American flag at public places in the Zone, including in front of Balboa High School—the school inside the Canal Zone attended by American students. This intransigence on the part of American youth sparked a response by Panamanian students, who, on the afternoon of January 9, marched into the Canal Zone to raise their flag alongside the U.S. colors in front of Balboa High School. Although these Panamanian students were actually carrying out the executive orders issued by Presidents Eisenhower and Kennedy, they met with violent resistance. Canal Zone police used tear gas and small arms to fend off Panamanian protestors, and that evening the Commander –in Chief of Southern Command took control of the Canal Zone police.

On the evening of January 9, the first Panamanian student was shot and killed by an American soldier, and the next morning President Chiari broke off diplomatic relations with the United States to protest the use of lethal force by American troops. The next three days witnessed a spectacular display of patriotism, bravery, and anger on the part of Panamanian students and other activists. By the time the *Guardia Nacional* occupied the area bordering the Canal Zone on January 13, two dozen young Panamanians had been killed by U.S. troops, and dozens more were seriously wounded.

Had Governor Fleming and other Canal Zone authorities obeyed the presidential order, history would have unfolded very differently. In the short term, the intransigence of Canal Zone authorities triggered a disastrous confrontation that would claim the lives of 24 Panamanian youth. In the long term, Fleming's decision to disregard the two presidential orders led directly to the renegotiation of the Panama Canal Treaty, a process that resulted in the Torrijos-Carter treaties of 1977.

October 1968

After the assassination of President José Remón in 1955, Panama's *Guardia Nacional* remained outside of the nation's limelight for the next decade. Remón's successor as Commander of the Guard, Colonel Bolívar Vallarino, was content to remain on the sidelines and allow the oligarchy to govern the nation. As the 1968 presidential election approached, however, the nation—and Vallarino—faced a dilemma. One candidate for president was Arnulfo Arias, the stridently nationalist archenemy of the National Guard. In 1941, and again in May 10, 1951, the Guardia Nacional had ousted Arias from the presidency; the 1951 incident is particularly significant because then Second Commander Bolívar Vallarino led the assault on the palace. Bolívar's troops won an hours-long firefight with Arias' followers before Arias finally surrendered the presidential palace.

In the course of the 1968 campaign, feuding among the oligarchy prevented them from coming up with an adequate opponent for Arias, who won the May 12 election and became President of Panama for the third time. Sworn into office on October 1, 1968, Arias immediately began to undertake a series of steps to restructure government in Panama City. One of his first steps was to begin the reorganization of the Guardia Nacional, including the forced retirement of Commander Bolívar Vallarino. Now a Brigadier General, Vallarino had the support of his junior officers, who vehemently opposed the president's interference in the affairs of the Guard.

On October 11, junior officers moved against Arias, taking over the palace and cutting off radio broadcasts in the capital. At the moment of the coup, Arias was in a movie theater a few miles from the palace, and initially he was unaware that he had been forcibly ousted from office. On learning of his fate, Arias had his driver take him through Panama City's back roads to the Canal Zone, where he went into exile. Joining him in the protection of the Americans were seven of the eight members of his cabinet and 24 members of the National Assembly.

In the months after Arias's ouster, the Guardia took a number of steps to cement its control of Panama's political system. Among other things, the Guard disbanded the National Assembly and all political parties. Officers also closed the Universidad de Panamá for several months to purge its faculty and student body of "subversives" who might foment unrest in that institution. The Guard also took control of Panama's media through censorship, management intervention, or outright expropriation.

For two months Colonel José María Pinilla, the Guard's ranking officer after Bolívar's retirement, filled the office of president. Pinilla promised Panamanians that his government was "provisional," and that elections were forthcoming after a brief period of stabilization. Real power behind the military junta actually rested with two charismatic junior officers, Omar Torrijos and Boris Martínez, commander and chief of staff of the Guard, respectively. Then in March, 1969, Martínez broadcast a speech to the nation wherein he promised agrarian reform and a series of other measures that seriously alarmed Panama's wealthy landowners. It alarmed Torrijos, too, who arrested Martínez and put him on a plane bound for permanent exile in Miami. Torrijos commented that Panama would be better off without Martínez; there would be "less impulsiveness" in government circles. Torrijos reassured the United States and Panama's wealthy landowners that their interests would be respected and protected.

Torrijos, now a brigadier general, survived an attempted coup in December 1969. During the next two years he moved slightly to the left, meticulously avoiding close association with Panama's Communist Party. He expressed his admiration for the socialist-styled military governments in Peru and Bolivia, and became known mostly as a populist. Reflecting the populist mode of thinking, in 1970 he stated, "Having finished with the oligarchy, the Panamanian has his own worth with no importance to his origin, his cradle, or where he was born."

In 1972, he enacted a new constitution and a sweeping new labor law that recognized the rights of working-class Panamanians. He actively sought the support of Panama's rural poor, and he enacted sweeping reforms in education and health care, establishing clinics throughout the countryside and requiring medical students to serve two-year internships at one of these rural clinics.

The Torrijos-Carter Treaties

General Torrijos's greatest accomplishment, though, was the negotiation of a new Panama Canal treaty with the United States. The negotiation process had begun in 1964 in the wake of the January 9 deaths of 24 Panamanian students. Richard Nixon had advanced the negotiation process when he reached a tentative agreement with Panama in the 1974 Tack-Kissinger agreement. Watergate delayed any definitive conclusion, however, so Panamanians waited until that crisis had settled. President Ford accelerated negotiations with Panama, and after the 1976 election, Torrijos and President Jimmy Carter moved the negotiating process forward. Carter eliminated the principal Panamanian concern when he agreed on a total withdrawal of U.S. military personnel from Panama, and the two sides quickly reached an agreement on September 7, 1977.

That day, two treaties were announced. The first treaty dealt with United States's administration of the canal during a gradual handover between 1977 and 1999. This treaty ended in December 1999 and was replaced by a second treaty that guaranteed perpetual neutrality of the canal. At this time, Panama took full control of the canal. This second treaty provides Washington the right to intervene militarily if the canal's security or neutrality is ever at risk. The second treaty will remain in effect as long as the canal exists

The signing of the Panama Canal treaties gave Torrijos a badly needed political victory. Panama's economy was a mess, and unrest was spreading throughout the republic. Over time, these social initiatives caused severe fiscal problems. By 1980, populist fiscal tactics used in the 1970s had created massive debt, and when Torrijos died in 1981, Panama had one of the highest per capita debts in the world and ranked third among Latin American nations for total indebtedness. In 1980, the external debt had reached 80 percent of GDP. These fiscal difficulties led inextricably to unemployment and social unrest, thus gradually eroding support for General Torrijos in some sectors.

Beyond his historic achievement with the Panama Canal treaties, General Torrijos had set out to correct Panama's skewed distribution of wealth, which in the 1960s was one of the worst in the world. In 1970, the richest 20 percent of Panama's population received 61.8 percent of the nation's income. Conversely, the poorest 20 percent of the population earned only 2 percent of income earned in the nation. By 1983, these numbers had changed markedly: the richest 20 percent of the population earned just over 50 percent of all income, while the poorest 20 percent of the population earned 3 percent of the nation's income. The three groups in between the two extremes made marked improvements, too, suggesting that Torrijos's policies did make income distribution in Panama more equitable. Nevertheless, most of the wealth remained entrenched in the cities, while the nation's rural population remained disproportionately impoverished.

After Torrijos: "Just Cause" and Democracy

After a two-year power struggle within the Guardia Nacional after Torrijos's death, Manuel Antonio Noriega became Panama's de facto ruler and military dictator. Like Torrijos, Noriega maintained a semblance of "democracy" by orchestrating elections where one or another of his close associates took a turn as president, but Noriega ruled unquestionably and mercilessly.

Noriega became Commander of the Guardia Nacional in August 1983 and immediately became a brigadier general. He then renamed the Guardia Nacional the *Fuerzas de Defensa de Panamá* (Panama Defense Forces—PDF). Noriega assumed the title of Commander –in Chief of the PDF. From this position, Noriega would dictate the nation's affairs for the next six years. As he assumed his new post, Noriega inherited an economy and a society reeling after 15 years of populist economic uncertainty, including massive domestic and foreign debts that limited the government's ability to spend. Unlike Torrijos, Noriega was not a charismatic ideologue, and he would not have the money to create jobs and make improvements as Torrijos had done.

When Noriega assumed leadership of the PDF, Panama's private sector was stagnating, the public sector was enormous, and private investment was waning. Meanwhile, the nation's GDP between 1980 and 1983 rose only 3.3 percent.

Foreign creditors and the International Monetary Fund demanded that Noriega take drastic, austere measures to enable Panama to meet its debt responsibilities. Meanwhile, Noriega's own dealings with the United States and with Colombian narcotics traffickers brought intense international scrutiny, further exacerbating the oligarchy's disdain for the increasingly unpopular regime.

Further accentuating the erosion of support for the Noriega dictatorship, during the late 1980s, more than 100 student groups protested, some violently, against the regime's flagrant disregard for human rights and its suspension of the most basic constitutional rights of the nation's citizenry. Noriega's reliance on the *Fuerzas de Defensa* to repress political opposition further alienated students and others opponents of the regime. The 1985 murder of Noriega's outspoken political opponent, Hugo Spadafora, left little doubt regarding the lengths to which the government would go to quell opposition. This became painfully clear during the presidential elections of 1989, when in the process of "defending" Panama's sovereignty, Noriega's forces attacked opposition candidate Guillermo Endara and his running mates. In a stunning display of violent political repression, the opposition candidates were beaten on international television and one of their bodyguards, Alexis Guerra, was killed. By the time U.S. troops invaded Panama in December 1989, Noriega's circle of support had shrunk to include primarily sectors of the poor working neighborhoods (*barriadas*) that surround the capital city, most notably the massive shanty-town community of San Miguelito, located on the outskirts of Panama City.

In the 1960s and 1970s, Noriega had been on the payroll of the Central Intelligence Agency, as an informant while yet a junior officer in Panama's *Guardia Nacional*. He had worked closely with U.S. officials at the School of the Americas when it was located in Panama, and in the 1980s he allowed American forces to use Panama as a staging ground in the U.S. war against Communist forces in Central America. By the mid-1980s, however, Noriega had outlived his usefulness. American officials had ignored Noriega's penchant for drug trafficking because he had proven a useful asset to the American military and intelligence establishments. In 1986, stories emerged regarding Noriega's complicity in drug trafficking and money laundering, and, in 1988, a Florida grand jury indicted Noriega on charges of racketeering and drug trafficking.

Noriega responded to these charges with increased repression and political intimidation in Panama, and, in 1989, Noriega's problems reached a crescendo. On October 3, Major Moisés Giroldi Vega, one of Noriega's staunch supporters within the PDF, attempted a coup to forcibly remove Noriega from office. At one point Giroldi actually held Noriega hostage at gunpoint while waiting for an American helicopter he hoped would arrive to carry the general into exile. When no outside support arrived, Giroldi put down his weapon and Noriega had him captured, tortured, and executed. The October 3 coup attempt ended in failure and various officers who conspired (or were believed to have conspired) were also tortured and executed.

The next month, things got worse for the general. On December 19, 1989, more than 20,000 U.S. troops invaded Panama and began the search for Noriega, now an indicted criminal in the United States. For two weeks U.S. troops engaged PDF forces and went house –by house in some areas in search of the elusive General Noriega. Eventually U.S. commanders became aware that Noriega had sought asylum in the Vatican embassy in Panama City (the *nunciatura*). American troops encircled the Vatican compound and carried out a game of psychological cat-and-mouse, playing loud rock music around the clock while addressing Noriega over a public address system. Eventually, Noriega broke and surrendered to U.S. authorities on January 3, 1990. That same evening U.S. Drug Enforcement Agency personnel took custody of Noriega and flew him to Homestead Air Force Base in Miami. Convicted of drug trafficking in 1992, Noriega was sentenced to 40 years in prison, a sentence that has since been reduced to 30 years.

Return to Civilian Government

The 1989 invasion of Panama ended two decades of rule by military dictatorships in Panama. Guillermo Endara Galimany, an attorney with training in Panama and the United States, won the 1989 election, which was subsequently annulled by Noriega's forces. When U.S. troops invaded in 1989, they took Endara to a U.S. military base and installed him as the President of Panama. Although he had won the popular vote, the circumstances surrounding Endara's ascension to the presidency forever marked him as a Washington lackey. Significantly, Endara abolished the nation's armed forces on February 10, 1994. In October of that year, the legislative assembly approved a constitutional amendment abolishing the army.

In the 1994 election, the Panamanian electorate returned to power Torrijos's *Partido Revolucionario Democrático* (Democratic Revolutionary Party—PRD) when PRD candidate Ernesto Pérez Balladares won the presidency. Since then, the *Arnulfistas* and the PRD have literally taken turns occupying the presidency. In the 1999 election, the Arnulfistas nominated Arnulfo Arias's widow, Mireya Moscoso, who became the nation's first female president. Then, in 2004, General Torrijos' son, Martín Torrijos Espino, ran successfully for president as the PRD candidate.

Panama has experienced not only profound political but also economic changes since 1989. On December 31, 1999, Panama assumed full sovereign control of the Panama Canal. Having adjusted to the loss of income caused by the withdrawal of thousands of American troops, Panama is doing a superb job owning and operating its canal. The nation is preparing to widen the locks to allow more transits, and it has attracted considerable private investment along the canal, selling off port services, for example, to large multinational corporations such as Hutchinson-Whampoa. The government is also expanding its ecotourism trade, which accounts for tens of millions of dollars each year. Meanwhile, although Panama's GDP dropped to 0.2 percent in 2002, it rose to 3.2 percent the next year. Despite 14 percent unemployment in 2003, Panama has the highest GDP in all of Central America.

8

Central America in the Twenty-First Century

The end of the twentieth century marked a historical juncture in the history of Central America. The cold war had ended, U.S. troops had withdrawn entirely from Panama, and the civil wars that had torn apart El Salvador, Guatemala, Honduras, and Nicaragua had drawn to their respective conclusions. Despite these remarkable changes, it would be an error to suggest that Central America has "redemocratized." Indeed, most of the problems that sparked the violence of the 1970s and 1980s still exist. Widespread poverty and desperation continue to plague the majority of Central Americans while the very wealthiest citizens of each nation remain intently focused on protecting their interests.

The real test of the peace in much of Central America will be how each nation responds in the event of a severe economic crisis. Sharp decreases in world coffee prices over the past several years have forced five of the seven nations of Central America (Panama and Belize excepted) to expand and diversify their economies in order to survive. Costa Rica has the advantage in this area, as it is not recovering from a brutal civil war and thus does not have a problem with investor confidence. At the other end of the spectrum, Guatemala has perhaps the furthest to go in terms of investor confidence; its bloody civil war ended in 1996, and ongoing violence and political scandals continue to plague investor confidence.

WHAT CAN THE PAST TEACH US ABOUT CENTRAL AMERICA'S FUTURE?

Regarding the Central American Free Trade Agreement (CAFTA), Costa Rica has diversified and thrived economically without it, and the Costa Rican economy has for years attracted large multinational investors looking to do business in tropical America. Conversely, Guatemala's situation and its economy must stabilize further before the nation is ready to capitalize on free trade with its neighbors. In its current condition, few companies, domestic or foreign, seem eager to take the risk of investing in Guatemala. Beyond these concerns, Guatemala's educational system must become more inclusive to increase its literacy rate so that it can provide a more educated work force—another necessary factor in attracting investment (Table 8.1).

Nicaragua's literacy rate is actually lower than that of Guatemala, but Nicaragua's postwar reconstruction has advanced further, and it has more investment and fewer violent flare-ups that does Guatemala. Most notably, Nicaragua has held free and democratic elections since 1989 without the problems that continue plaguing Guatemala nine years after the peace accord officially ended Guatemala's civil war. Finally, an increasing number of students in Nicaragua are receiving technical training that will equip them to work in fields such as computer science and engineering. This training, combined with more emphasis on training the nation's teachers, will ensure that economic diversification can proceed and accelerate. As demonstrated by the data in Table 8.2, Nicaragua remains the hemisphere's second poorest nation—second only to Haiti. However, its potential for growth and well-being for its citizens is great. Nicaragua has reached a crossroads and appears ready to move beyond its troubled recent past.

Table 8.1   Literacy in the Central American Republics, 2004*

Belize	Costa Rica	El Salvador	Guatemala	Honduras	Nicaragua	Panama
94.1%	96%	80.2%	70%	76.2%	67.5%	92.6%

* In this data, "literacy" is defined as persons ages 15 years and older who can read and write.

Two Central American nations, Belize and Panama, are not part of CAFTA. Their economies are sufficiently different from those of the other Central American countries that they face their own unique –but related challenges. Both are striving to sustain economic diversification, and both face their own challenges. In Belize, the government enacted a series of financial policies in September 1998 that have resulted in excellent growth for the economy. Between 1999 and 2004, Belize's gross domestic product (GDP) grew an average of 6 percent annually.[1] Although that growth slowed some through 2004, Belize's economy continues to be stable and, therefore, attractive to investment. Tourism continues to be Belize's principal source of income, but over many years it has diversified to include textile manufacturing in addition to the more traditional sources of income—marine exports and tropical goods including sugar and bananas. With little vested interest in the coffee industry, recent price declines in that crop have had no effect on Belize.

Panama's economy revolves around its enormous service sector, which produces 80 percent of its GDP. These services include operation of the Panama Canal, banking, the Colon Free Zone, insurance, container ports, flagship registry, and tourism. Since assuming full control of the canal in 1999, Panama has expanded and diversified each facet of the service sector. Panama's tourism industry, for example, has capitalized on its ownership and control of the canal to expand exponentially the nation's ecotourism. A thriving tourism industry—complete with luxury hotels, transportation, hotels, restaurants, ground and air transportation, and medical care—has emerged on lands once occupied by U.S. military bases. Beginning in 2004, the Panamanian government began offering lucrative tax incentives to investors from all over the world, with the result that Panama's export industry and construction industry have begun growing rapidly.

Foreign investors find Panama's educated, skilled work force and its control of the world's preeminent waterway enticing incentives to settle in Panama and to do business there. Unemployment

Table 8.2 Gross Domestic Product Per Capita (2004) (in U.S. dollars)

Belize	Costa Rica	El Salvador	Guatemala	Honduras	Nicaragua	Panama
$6,500	$9,600	$4,900	$4,200	$2,800	$2,300	$6,900

Table 8.3 Life Expectancy in Central America (2004)

Belize	Costa Rica	El Salvador	Guatemala	Honduras	Nicaragua	Panama
68 years	77 years	72 years	65 years	66 years	70 years	72 years

continues to hover between 12 and 13 percent, but the economic trends of the first years of the twenty-first century suggest that Panama is primed to become the economic and technological power to be reckoned with among the Central American nations.

In modern Central America, available economic and social indicators suggest a relationship among several factors that constitute the fabric of daily life in each of the seven nations:

stable civil government → economic development → better lives

As suggested by the comparative demographic data contained in Table 8.3, Central America's recent history suggests that when governments behave civilly, they promote economic well-being, which in turn fosters improved living conditions for the population. Conversely, history is replete with examples of what happens when this "civil government" model breaks down. Dictators greedily use violence to pursue their interest, terrorizing populations and scaring off any potential investment, resulting in lower wages, higher unemployment, and increased human suffering. The few social indicators presented in this chapter would seem to corroborate these conclusions.

On the surface, this proposal seems to promote capitalism and to denigrate alternative economic models. It is true that the Nicaraguan experiment in Communist economics certainly failed miserably, but the Costa Rican model contradicts such oversimplifications. On the one hand, Costa Rica has a long history of open, democratic elections, successful civilian rule, and completion of constitutionally mandated terms. On the other hand, its social security program enables the federal government to tax and use those funds for medical care, education, and other social programs aimed at improving daily life for all Costa Ricans. Even during the cold war, Costa Rica maintained its neutrality and preserved the integrity of its national borders: no foreign troops occupied Costa Rica in the name of fighting (or promoting) capitalism or communism. Hence, Costa Rica provides us a glowing exception to the extremist "capitalist-or-communist" mentality so prevalent elsewhere in Central America.

The future of each of the seven Central American nations hinges on a variety of complex factors that will help shape their futures. First, each must continue their current pursuit of sustainable economic well-being. This requires governments to continue to court international investment and to promote investment by their own residents. CAFTA may or may not assist in this process, but if any government fails to ratify it, the governments of participating nations will have to find other ways to promote investment, production, and exports.

Second, elected civilian governments will need to clearly outline the role of their respective militaries within the broader society. Costa Rica and Panama have now accomplished this by disbanding their militaries altogether, which has helped prevent military intervention when financial and political difficulties arise. The other Spanish-speaking nations of Central America must follow suit.

Finally, the political systems of each country must mature to the point that Costa Rica has reached. There, aggressive opponents of the government constitute a legitimate part of the official political process; they have a voice in their country's political decisions. With their civil wars still in recent memory, El Salvador, Guatemala, and Nicaragua must aggressively take steps to ensure that the political opposition remains actively involved in the nation's day-to-day functions. In Nicaragua, for example, the *Frente Sandinista de Liberación Nacional* (Sandinista National Liberation Front, FSLN) continues to participate in federal and regional elections. Serious splits within the FSLN have occurred since 1989, however, and Daniel Ortega continues to insist that he dominate the group's political processes. In early 2005, he used his still-considerable influence within the FSLN to force the party to nominate him as their candidate in the next presidential election still a year away. This extraordinary step has angered the reformists in the FSLN who believe he has led the group astray and is responsible for their loss of power. This is an extraordinarily dangerous situation that could trigger violent infighting among the Sandinistas, which, in turn, may spill over into national politics should the economy slow down drastically.

Accomplishing these three things will not ensure that a Central American nation does not revert to a violent civil war. Ethnic hatred (Guatemala), natural disasters, and foreign military activities continue to be salient issues in the region. However, achieving success in these areas may enable Central American governments to withstand severe crises such as hurricanes. Honduras provides an excellent example of this political resiliency in the face of disaster. Its political system had evolved sufficiently that the nation survived Hurricane Mitch in 1998 without a military coup, without foreign military intervention, and without guerillas launching a war on the federal government.

NOTE

1. The U.S. Central Intelligence Agency defines GDP as the "value of all final goods and services produced within a nation in a given year."

Notable People in the History of Central America

Alvarado, Pedro de (1486–1541).   The most famous of Cortés's officers. Played an integral role in the defeat of the Aztec nation in 1519. Sent from Mexico by Hernán Cortes in 1524 to conquer Central America. There he allied himself with Cachikeles to conquer the Quiché, which he accomplished in 1524. Among the most ruthless and bloodthirsty of the *conquistadores*; renown for his viciousness.

Arbenz, Jacobo (1913–1971).   Progressive president of Guatemala 1950–1954. Ousted by CIA-backed coup in 1954, which terminated reforms perpetuated by Arbenz and his predecessor, Juan José Arévalo. At his ouster, Carlos Castillo Armas became president of Guatemala with Washington's support. Returned Guatemala to conservative rule and served as president until his assassination in 1957.

Arias, Arnulfo (1901–1988).   Elected president of Panama four times, each time was ousted by the National Guard shortly into his administration. As Panama's minister to Italy during the period 1934–1938, became increasingly attracted to the Europe's totalitarian dictatorships. After his election in 1940, enacted a radically conserva-tive constitution that mirrored his pro-Hitler attitude: the constitution enacted in January 1941 prohibited the immigration to Panama of "racially and ethnically parasitic races" including Jewish Syrians and Blacks "whose native language is not Spanish." Prohibited the granting of business licenses to all "prohibited races."

Aspinwall, William Henry (1807–1875).   American financier and managing agent of the Pacific Mail Steamship Company during the California gold rush. Secretly devised a plan for a railroad across Panama to speed the journey between California and the eastern seaboard of the United States. Dream came to fruition in January 1855, when his Panama Railroad traveled from Colón on the east coast to Panama City on the west coast, thereby cementing his place in history and galvanizing Panama's role in the emerging economy.

Asturias, Miguel Angel (1899–1974).   Prolific Guatemalan author in the "Magical Realism" movement. Put Central America firmly on the map of worldwide literature. Translated the sacred Mayan text, Popul Vuh, from French to Spanish in 1927.

Balboa, Vasco Núñez de (1475–1519).   Stowaway member of Bastidas's 1501 crew; "discovered" the Pacific ocean for the Europeans in September 1513. Beheaded by his archenemy Pedro de Arias Dávila in 1519.

Barrios, Justo Rufino (1835–1885).   Liberal who helped end decades of conservative rule. Became dictator of Guatemala in 1873 and ruled with an iron fist until his assassination in 1885. During his reign, reinstated onerous vagrancy laws aimed at forcibly con-trolling and exploiting the region's large indigenous population.

Bastidas, Rodrigo de (1460–1527).   Led an expedition to the east coast of South America in 1500. His party included Vasco Núñez de Balboa. First European to set foot on Central American soil, coming ashore at Panama's Nombre de Dios in March 1501.

Calderón Guardia, Rafael Angel (1900–1970).   Reform-minded president of Costa Rica, 1940–1944. Joined forces with Costa Rica's Communist Party and enacted a series of sweeping progressive legislation, including the establishment of Costa Rica's social security program.

Carías Andino, Tiburcio (1876–1969). "Velvet-gloved" military dictator of Honduras from 1932 to 1948. Less ruthless than his colleagues in El Salvador, Nicaragua, and Guatemala. Close affiliation with the United Fruit Company enabled him to partially assuage the concerns and needs of the working poor; close alliance with a large foreign company also placated the nation's tiny wealthy oligarchy. Somewhat like Rafael Carrera in the nineteenth century, achieved an odd, uneasy balance with the various sectors of Honduran society.

Carrera, Rafael (1814–1865). Conservative Central American *caudillo* who came to power as a result of the Mountain War in the late 1830s. Dominated Central American politics from 1839 to 1865, serving as "Perpetual President of Guatemala" until his death in 1865. Conservative dictator who successfully balanced conservative and liberal tendencies, in large measure because demand for Guatemalan materials remained high throughout his reign.

Columbus, Christopher (1451–1506). Explored Central America's Caribbean coast on his fourth voyage (1502).

Dávila, Pedrarias (aka Pedro Arias de Ávila; 1440–1531). Established Panama City in 1519. Brutally exploited Indians, enslaving and murdering them while exploiting their labor, raw materials, and possessions. In 1528, Pedrarias proposed an interoceanic route across Nicaragua, preferring that path over the Panama route.

DeLesseps, Ferdinand (1805–1894). Frenchman who dug the Suez Canal across Egypt, having successfully completed that project in 1869. Established French Compagnie Universelle du Canal Interocéanique, which began digging a pathway across Panama in 1881. Effort ended in failure in 1889 when the company went broke because of graft and poor management; DeLesseps died in disgrace in France in December 1894.

Drake, Francis (1540–1596). English buccaneer/pirate who repeatedly assaulted Central America's coastline in the latter half of the sixteenth century. Most audacious exploits involved the sacking of Panama's Nombre de Dios, transit point for gold and silver en route to Europe. Died off Panama's coast in January 1596 and is buried there on a tiny island off the coast of Portobelo, Panama.

Ferrera, Francisco (1794–1851). Conservative ally of Rafael Carrera. Dominated Honduran politics 1839 to 1847.

Figueres Ferrer, José (1906–1990). Leader of the successful 1948 movement to overthrow the liberal Calderón Guardia government of Costa Rica, which launched Figueres's domination of the nation's political system, where he served as president on three separate occasions (once as interim chief of state after the revolution). More recently, his son, José María Figueres Olsen, served one term as president of Costa Rica (1994–1998).

Gerardi, Monsignor Juan José (1922–1998). Guatemalan Bishop whose group, Recovery of the Historic Memory Project, published a scathing report on human rights abuses in Guatemala. Two days after this report was published in 1998, he was bludgeoned to death by an assailant wielding a brick.

Guardia, Tomás (1832–1882). Costa Rican military dictator in the 1870s. Promoted foreign investment and progressive reforms including universal education and banning the death penalty. Wrote the 1871 constitution, which remained in effect until 1994.

Hanyes, Samuel (1898–1971). Important Belizean labor leader in 1919 who penned the nation's national anthem, "Land of the Free."

Hernández Martínez, Maximiliano (1882–1966). General in the army of El Salvador. Became president in a coup in late 1931, and as president ordered the Matanza massacre, which killed 30,000 persons in January 1932. Brutal military dictator who defended El Salvador's coffee elite at the expense of the remainder of the nation.

Las Casas, Bartolomé de (1484–1566). Dominican priest, author, and activist. Came to the New World in 1502 as one of the conquistadores. Received his first *encomienda* (land grants with Indians) when he helped quell an uprising among indigenous population. After his ordination to the Dominican Order, served as chaplain during the pacification of Cuba, for which he received another *encomienda*. In 1514, renounced his *encomiendas* and denounced Spanish treatment of indigenous peoples. Thus began his struggle against European aggression in the New World, a battle he fought for the rest of his life. An accomplished author, Las Casas' most influential work, "A Brief Report on the Destruction of the Indians," provided a scathing rebuke of European abuses in the Americas. Widely revered as the "champion of the Indian," but must be seen in his sixteenth-century context. Opposed to the exploitation of Indians, but he favored using Blacks from Africa to do the Europeans' manual labor in the New World.

Martí, Agustín Farabundo (1893–1932). Communist guerilla fighter in El Salvador in the 1930s. Helped organize and lead strikes in El Salvador's coffee region in late 1931, which ultimately resulted in La Matanza, the military's brutal slaying of thousands of rural peasants. Executed in February 1932.

Mora Valverde, Manuel (1909–1994). Founder of the Costa Rican Communist Party in 1931. When the Communist Party disbanded later in the 1930s, helped organize the Popular Vanguard in 1943 to help establish a broader base than he had been able to achieve with the Communist Party.

Morazán, Francisco (1799–1842). Honduran liberal leader in 1820s and 1830s. Became President of the United Provinces of Central America in 1830 and enacted a series of liberal reforms aimed at reforming the church, land distribution, education, and the judicial system. After the War of the Mountain in the late 1830s, conservative Guatemalan caudillo Rafael Carrera engaged Morazán and ultimately drove him from exile. When Morazán attempted to return in 1842, he was captured and executed.

Morgan, Henry (1635–1688). Pirate/buccaneer who attacked various Central American communities; attacked and burned Panama City in 1671.

Noriega, Manuel Antonio (1938–). Commander of Panama's Defense Forces (1983–1989). Indicted for narcotics trafficking in a Miami court in 1987, and in 1989 was apprehended by American troops during the U.S. invasion of Panama, an operation called,

"Just Cause." Convicted in 1992 and sentenced to 40 years in a U.S. prison. Sentence was later reduced to 30 years.

Ortega, Daniel (1945–).   Leader of Nicaragua's communist Frente *Sandinista de Liberación Nacional* (FSLN), which successfully ousted the Somoza government in 1979. President of Nicaragua until 1990; defeated in a presidential campaign by Violetta Chamorro, who became Nicaragua's first female president. Electoral defeat in 1990 marked a turning point for the FSLN, who continue to field candidates in the nation's elections in hopes of regaining the power they held in the 1980s. Ortega and his colleagues have a difficult time understanding why the people of Nicaragua rejected the FSLN.

Price, George (1919–).   Father of the nation of Belize. In the early 1960s, led Belize's campaign for independence from England. Unlike many of his peers, embraced the idea of a regional identity that linked Belize to its Spanish-speaking sister republics. Critics denounced him, claiming that he was promoting the "Latinization" of Belize. When Belize gained its independence from England in 1981, Price was the new nation's first prime minister.

Romero, Carlos Humberto (1924–).   General in Salvadoran army. President in late 1970s who carried out the "Public Order Law," which declared open season on civilians suspected of political intrigue.

Romero, Oscar (1917–1980).   Archbishop of El Salvador (1977–1980) whose promotion of civil rights in that country resulted in his murder in March 1980. Earlier in his career, had been an intellectual with little real-world experience. Conservative and did not initially embrace "liberation theology," arguing instead that the church ought to remain at the center of El Salvador's political situation. Shortly after becoming Archbishop, however, his best friend, Father Rutilio Grande, was assassinated by a government death squad. Then began his conversion to a more progressive, liberal worldview that ultimately led to his murder by a right-wing death squad.

Sandino, Augusto César (1895–1934).   Nationalist guerilla leader in Nicaragua who fought against occupying United States marines from 1928 until his murder in 1934. After his death other Nicaraguan patriots invoked his name in their ongoing struggle against U.S. intervention. Most recently, the *Frente Sandinista de Liberación*

Nacional (FSLN) won a civil war and governed the country for 10 years (1979–1989) until voters ousted the nation's FSLN president, Daniel Ortega.

Soberanis, Antonio (1897–1975).   Labor leader in Belize in the 1930s who declared he would, "rather be a dead hero than a living coward." Called Belize's merchants, "bloodsuckers," while referring to the governor and the king as "crooks." More than any other labor leader in Belize's history, Soberanis was the first person who articulated that nation's social and political problems. Attacked the Crown and questioned the need to have a colonial government. Also took his protests to the countryside, involving rural workers in the struggle for independence.

Somoza García, Anastasio (1896–1956).   First head of Nicaragua's National Guard, trained and equipped by the U.S. military. Assumed control of the country in 1934, was elected president in 1936, and remained in control until his assassination in 1956. Sons Luís and Anastasio Jr. continued conservative dictatorship until 1979 when the Sandinista revolution successfully ended their dynasty.

Tom, John Alexander.   Mahogany worker and labor organizer in Belize. Led the 1894 mahogany workers' strike, which resulted in higher wages for Belize's mahogany workers.

Torrijos Herrera, Omar (1929–1981).   Panamanian military officer who came to power in October 1968 as a result of a military coup. Effected myriad changes within Panamanian society, but his most lasting legacy are the Panama Canal treaties he signed with President Jimmy Carter in 1977. Died in a suspicious airplane crash in 1981; succeeded in power after some maneuvering by his intelligence chief, Manuel Noriega.

Urrutia y Montoya, Carlos (1750–1825).   Last Spanish Captain General of Central America (1818–1821). Rule ended in 1821 when Central America joined Mexico in declaring independence from Spain.

Walker, William (1824–1860).   American swashbuckler who intervened in the Nicaraguan army in 1855; made himself president in 1856.

Glossary of Foreign Language Words and Key Concepts

Armada del Sur: Name given to Spanish fleet that sailed along South America's Pacific Coast. This is how the Spaniards transported gods between the Andes and Panama.

Audiencia: Regional court in colonial Spanish America.

Bogotano: "From Bogotá," a person from Bogotá is a *Bogotano*.

Carrera de Indias: Literally, "Indies run." The fleet system that transported goods between Spain and America.

Caudillo: Political leader who leads using a combination of personal loyalty and fear; similar to a dictator. Most common in the nineteenth century, but a few ruled in the twentieth century.

Conquistador: Spanish conquerors, most notably the men who followed Cortés and Pizarro in the conquest and subjugation of the Aztec and Incan Empires.

Conservatives: People who favor restoring the church to its former prominence, oppose secularism, and favor powerful central government to protect individual rights.

Creole: A Spaniard born in the New World.

Death Squad: Professional political murderers. In Central America, death squad members frequently come from the ranks of the nation's police or military. Occasionally, conservative politicians use death squads to suppress opposition from workers and political enemies. Most common during times of economic and political unrest.

Encomienda: A system of tribute labor established in Spanish America. It gave the conquistador control over a piece of land and the indigenous peoples who lived on that land. The Indians living on the land were forced to pay tribute to the European *encomendero,* who in turn was required to provide shelter and spiritual training for the Indians.

Finca: A small farm.

Hispaniola: Name given by Spaniards to the island that is today the Dominican Republic and Haiti.

Isthmus: A narrow strip of land that connects two larger piece of land. Isthmians are people who live on an Isthmus, for example, Panama.

Junta: Military officers who seize power and take control of the government.

Liberals: People who promote weak central government, economic development, secular education, an influx of foreign investment, limiting the power of the church, and individualism.

Matanza: "Slaughter." Most notably, this is the name given to a huge massacre in El Salvador in 1932.

Mesoamerica: Area in southern Mexico and northern Central America where Maya and Olmec dwelt.

Mestizo: A person of mixed Indian and Spanish lineage.

Middle America: Another name for Central America, that stretch of land located between Mexico and South America.

Milpa: Mayan agricultural technique used to help increase nitrogen levels in soil. Very land-intensive, required Mayan families to move around a great deal.

Nationalism: Political movement based on national pride. In Latin America, nationalists oppose foreign intervention in the affairs of their nation.

Nombre de Dios: Colonial Spanish port on Panama's Caribbean coast.

Oligarchy: From Greek, "rule by the few." In the context of Central America, refers to a small group of powerful families who are able to control the government because of their influence and prestige. In the twentieth century, militaries and death squads frequently used force to protect the interests of these people. In return, police and military officials received frequently lucrative remuneration and favors.

Populist: Political movement that appeals to the urban working poor and middle class.

Portobelo: Panamanian coastal town; location of colonial Spain's Customs House.

Progressive: A liberal outlook that promotes progress, reform, and the protection of civil liberties.

Reforma: "Reform." Term used to describe the liberal reforms that occurred in the mid-nineteenth century in many Latin American countries. Liberal politicians "reformed" laws governing the church, land distribution, education, etc.

Regeneración: "Regeneration." Term used to describe the conservative resurgence in late-nineteenth century Colombia.

South Sea: Spanish name for the Pacific Ocean in the early sixteenth century.

Tehuantinsuyo: Inca homeland.

Tenochtitlán: Aztec capital city.

Teotihuacán: Large ancient city in Mexico.

Viceroyalty: Largest administrative unit in Spanish America. The Viceroy acted in place of the king of Spain and was thus the highest ranking colonial officer in the Americas.

Yucatán: Refers to the Yucatán Peninsula in Southern Mexico/northernmost Central America, where Maya thrived and where Europeans came ashore during their conquest.

Central American History: A Bibliographic Essay

BELIZE

On the roots of labor unrest in modern Belize, see Mark Moberg, *Myths of Ethnicity and Nation: Immigration, Work, and Identity in the Belize Banana Industry* (Knoxville, 1997). Regarding resistance to British rule in Belize, see O. Nigel Bolland's new work, *Colonialism and Resistance in Belize: Essays in Historical Sociology* (Kingston, 2004). Regarding the formation of an independent Belize, see Narda Dobson's general *History of Belize* (London, 1973); O. Nigel Bolland, *The Formation of a Colonial Society* (Baltimore, 1977) and *Belize: A New Nation in Central America* (Boulder, 1986); Wayne Clegern, *British Honduras, Colonial Dead End, 1859–1900* (Baton Rouge, 1967); C . H. Grant, *The Making of Modern Belize* (Cambridge, 1976); Liter Hunter Krohn, et al. (eds.) *Readings in Belizean History* (2d ed., Belize City, 1987). See also Ann Sutherland's new work on Belize, *The Making of Belize* (Westport, 1998).

COSTA RICA

Two fine starting points are Lowell Gudmundson's important work, *Costa Rica before Coffee: Society and Economy on the Eve of the*

Export Boom (Baton Rouge, 1986) and Charles D. Ameringer, *Don Pepe: Political Biography of José Figueres of Costa Rica* (Albuquerque, 1978).

On land distribution and money in Costa Rica, see Marc Edelman, *The Logic of the Latifundio: The Large Estates of Northwestern Costa Rica since the Late Nineteenth Century* (Stanford, 1992). Regarding the United Fruit Company's use of West Indian labor in Limón, see Aviva Chomsky, *West Indian Workers and the United Fruit Company in Costa Rica, 1870–1940* (Baton Rouge, 1996). The definitive work on Costa Rica's 1948 revolution remains John. P. Bell's classic work on the 1948 revolution, *Crisis in Costa Rica: The 1948 Revolution* (Austin, 1971). See also Bruce Wilson, *Costa Rica: Politics, Economics, and Democracy* (Boulder, 1998), and Carolyn Hall *Costa Rica, A Geographical Interpretation in Historical Perspective* (Boulder, 1985). On American entrepreneur and railroad builder Minor C. Keith in Costa Rica, see *Keith of Costa Rica: A Biographic Study of Minor Cooper Keith* (Albuquerque, 1974).

EL SALVADOR

A fine starting place for recent events in El Salvador is Enrique Baloyra, *El Salvador in Transition* (Chapel Hill, 1982).

Regarding land, economics, and social class in El Salvador, see Aldo Lauria-Santiago, *An Agrarian Republic: Commercial Agriculture and the Politics of Peasant Communities in El Salvador, 1823–1914* (Pittsburgh, 1999). For information on the 1981 massacre, see Thomas F. Anderson, *Matanza: El Salvador's Communist Revolt of 1932* (2d ed., Williamantic, Conn., 1992), and *The War of the Dispossessed* (Lincoln, 1981); David Browning, *El Salvador, Landscape and Society* (Oxford, 1971); Hugh Byrne, *El Salvador's Civil War: A study of Revolution* (Boulder, 1996) on the 1969 "soccer war." Also on the 1969 war, see William Durham, *Scarcity and Survival in Central America: Ecological Origins of the Soccer War* (Stanford, 1979). More recently, see James. A. Dunkerley, *The Long War: Dictatorship and Revolution in El Salvador* (London, 1982); Philip Russell, *El Salvador in Crisis* (Austin, 1984); Tommie Sue Montgomery, *Revolution in El Salvador: From Civil Strife to Civil Peace* (2d ed., Boulder, 1995); Philip Williams and Knut Walter, *Militarization and Demilitarization in El Salvador's Transition to Democracy* (Pittsburgh, 1997); and Joseph Tulchin and Gary Bland, *Is There a Transition to Democracy in El Salvador?* (Boulder, 1992).

On Archbishop Oscar Romero, see James Brockman, *Romero: A Life* (Maryknoll, New York, 2003).

Finally, on political violence in El Salvador in the 1970s and 1980s, see Belisario Betancur, et al., *From Madness to Hope: The 12-Year War in El Salvador: Report of the Commission on the Truth for El Salvador* (United Nations, 1993); and Leigh Binford, *The El Motoze Massacre: Anthropology and Human Rights* (Tucson, 1996).

GUATEMALA

Two outstanding books to begin with are Nancy Farris's monumental *Maya Society under Colonial Rule: The Collective Enterprise of Survival* (Princeton, 1984) and David J. McCreery, *Rural Guatemala, 1760–1940* (Stanford, 1994).

From there, see Jim Handy's superb *Gift of the Devil, A History of Guatemala* (Boston, 1984) and his more recent *Revolution in the Countryside: Rural Conflict & Agrarian Reform in Guatemala, 1944–1954* (Chapel Hill, 1994); Paul Dosal, *Power in Transition: The Rise of Guatemala's Industrial Oligarchy, 1871–1994* (Westport, Conn., 1995), and *Doing Business with the Dictators: A Political History of United Fruit in Guatemala, 1899–1944* (Wilmington, Del., 1993). Also see Kenneth J. Grieb, *Guatemalan Caudillo: the Regime of Jorge Ubico, 1931–1944* (Athens, Ohio, 1979); Piero Gleijeses's important work, *Shattered Hope: The Guatemalan Revolution and the United States, 1944–1954* (Princeton, 1991); Richard Adams's classic *Crucifixion by Power: Essays on Guatemalan Social Structure, 1944–1966* (Austin, 1970); Robert Carmack (ed.), *Harvest of Violence: The Maya Indians and the Guatemalan Crisis* (Norman, 1988), which describes recent government repression of the Maya community; Rigoberta Menchú's controversial, *I, ... Rigoberta Menchú: An Indian Woman in Guatemala* (London, 1984); David Stoll's critique of Menchú's book, *Rigoberta Menchú and the Story of All Poor Guatemalans;* Susanne Jonas, *The Battle for Guatemala: Rebels, Death Squads, and U.S. Power* (Boulder, 1991); and Richard Immerman's important study, *The CIA in Guatemala* (Austin, 1983).

HONDURAS

On Spanish-Indian relations in Honduras, see Linda Newsome, *The Cost of Conquest: Indian Decline in Honduras under Spanish Rule* (Boulder, 1986). On economics in late nineteenth-century Honduras, see Kenneth Finney, *In Quest of El Dorado: Precious Metal Mining and the Modernization of Honduras, 1880–1900* (New York, 1987). On militarism in Honduras, see James. A. Morris, *Honduras: Caudillo Politics and Military Rulers* (Boulder, 1984), and Darío Euraque, *Reinterpreting the Banana Republic: Region & State in Honduras, 1870–1972* (Chapel Hill, 1997). On the "Soccer War," see Thomas P. Anderson, *War of the Dispossessed: Honduras and El Salvador, 1969* (Lincoln, 1982).

NICARAGUA

For two decades Nicaragua was a "six-o'clock news" country that received considerable attention in the English-language press. Foremost among the books on revolution are Neill Macaulay's critical book, *The Sandino Affair* (2d ed., Durham, N. C., 1985), and Jeffrey Gould's two excellent contributions, *To Lead as Equals: Rural Protest* and *Political Consciousness in Chinandega, Nicaragua, 1912–1979* (Chapel Hill, 1990). William Kamman, *A Search for Stability, 1925–1933* (Notre Dame, Ind., 1968); Richard Millet, *Guardians of the Dynasty* (Maryknoll, N.Y., 1977); Knut Walter, *The Regime of Anastasio Somoza* (Chapel Hill, 1993); and Shirley Christian's *Revolution in the Family* (New York, 1986) all provide useful context within which to consider the Sandinista movement. See also Harry Vanden and Gary Prevost, *Democracy and Socialism in Sandinista Nicaragua* (Boulder, 1992); John Booth, *The End and the Beginning* (2d ed., Boulder, 1985); David Nolan, *FSLN: The Ideology of the Sandinistas and the Nicaraguan Revolution* (Miami, 1984); Dennis Gilbert, *The Sandinistas: The Party and the Revolution* (Oxford, 1988); Rose Spalding, *Capitalists and Revolution in Nicaragua: Opposition and Accommodation, 1979–1993* (Chapel Hill, 1994); and Mark Everingham, *Revolution and the Multiclass Coalition in Nicaragua* (Pittsburgh, 1996). On the peace process, see James Dunkerley, *The Pacification of Central America: Political Change in the Isthmus, 1987–1993* (London, 1994). See also Jeffrey Gould's *To Die This Way: Nicaraguan Indians and the Myth of Mestizaje, 1880–1965* (Durham, 1998).

PANAMA

The most important English-language work on colonial Panama is Christopher Ward's superb, *Imperial Panama: Commerce and Conflict in Isthmian America, 1550–1800* (Albuquerque, 1993).

See also Alex Pérez-Venero, *Before the Five Frontiers: Panama from 1821–1903* (New York, 1978); Gerstle Mack, *The Land Dividend* (New York, 1994); Lancelot S. Lewis, *The West Indian in Panama, 1850–1914* (Washington, 1980); John and Mavis Biesanz, *The People of Panama* (New York, 1955). The most important work on the early years of the twentieth century is Gustavo Mellander, *The United States in Panamanian Politics: The Intriguing Formative Years* (Danville, 1971). Also, on the formative years in Panama see Peter Szok's fine new book, *"La última gaviota": Liberalism and Nostalgia in Early Twentieth-Century Panama* (Westport, 2001). On the military and politics in Panama, see Steve Ropp's masterful work, *Panamanian Politics: From Guarded Nation to National Guard* (Stanford, 1982) and Margaret Scranton, *The Noriega Years: U.S.-Panamanian Relations, 1981–1990* (Boulder, 1991). See also Carlos Guevera Mann, *Panamanian Militarism: A Historical Interpretation* (Athens, Ohio, 1996), and Thomas L. Pearcy, *We Answer Only to God: Politics and the Military in Panama, 1903–1947* (Albuquerque, 1998).

The definitive work on the canal remains David McCullough's *Path Between the Seas: The Creation of the Panama Canal, 1870–1914* (New York, 1977). See also Michael Conniff's superb work, *Black Labor on a White Canal* (Pittsburgh, 1985), Walter LaFeber, *The Panama Canal: The Crisis in Historical Perspective* (3d ed., New York, 1989); and John Major, *Prize Possession: The United States and the Panama Canal, 1903–1979* (Cambridge, 1993).

On General Omar Torrijos, see Sharon Phillipps Collazos, *Labor and Politics in Panama: The Torrijos Years* (Boulder, 1991), and George Priestly, *Government and Popular Participation in Panama: The Torrijos Regime, 1968–1975* (Boulder, 1986). See also Andrew Zimbalist and John Weeks, *Panama at the Crossroads: Economic Development and Political Change in the Twentieth Century* (Berkeley, 1991), and Robert C. Harding, *Military Foundations of Panamanian Politics* (New Brunswick, 2001).

GENERAL HISTORICAL SURVEYS

Histories of the Region

The place to begin is Ralph Lee Woodward's comprehensive *Central America: A Nation Divided* (3d ed. New York, 1999). See also

Steve C. Ropp and James A. Morris, editors, *Central America: Crisis and Adaptation* (Albuquerque, 1984).

For an excellent book by a fine Central American scholar consult Héctor Pérez Brignoli, *A Brief History of Central America* (Berkeley, 1989). For an excellent discussion of society in Central America, see Richard Adams, *Cultural Surveys of Panama-Nicaragua-Guatemala-El Salvador-Honduras* (Washington, D.C., 1957). See also Jeffrey Paige, *Coffee and Power: Revolution and the Rise of Democracy in Central America* (Cambridge, Mass., 1997), Robert Williams in *States and Social Evolution: Coffee and the Rise of National Governments in Central America* (Chapel Hill, 1994), and Costa Rican scholar Samuel Stone's wonderful, *Heritage of the Conquistadors: Ruling Classes in Central America from Conquest to the Sandinistas* (Lincoln, 1990).

See also Lowell Gudmundson and Hector Lindo-Fuentes, *Central America, 1821–1871; Liberalism before Liberal Reform* (Tuscaloosa, 1995), and Gudmundson, William Roseberry, and Mario S. Kutschbach, editors, *Coffee, Society, and Power in Central America* (Baltimore, 1995).

For more in-depth treatment of Central American history generally see Murdo MacLeod's classic *Spanish Central America: A Socioeconomic History, 1520–1720* (Berkeley, 1973). See also Miles Wortman, *Government and Society in Central America, 1680–1840* (N.Y., 1982); James Dunkerley, *Power in the Isthmus, A Political History of Modern Central America* (London, 1988); Victor Bulmer-Thomas, *The Political Economy of Central America since 1920* (Cambridge, 1987).

Books That Focus on the Nineteenth Century

Mario Rodríguez, *The Cádiz Experiment in Central America, 1808–1826* (Berkeley, 1978); Thomas L. Karnes, *Failure of Union, Central America, 1824–1975* (2d ed., Tempe, Az., 1975), Douglass Sullivan-González, *Piety, Power, and Politics: Religion and Nation-Formation in Guatemala, 1821–1871* (Pittsburgh, 1998); and Ralph Lee Woodward, *Rafael Carrera and the Emergence of the Republic of Guatemala, 1821–71* (Athens, Ga., 1993) focus on the conservative dictatorship of Rafael Carrera in Guatemala. Lowell Gudmundson, *Costa Rica Before Coffee: Society and Economy on the Eve of Export Boon* (Baton Rouge, 1986) explains the early development of the Costa Rican rural society and its elite.

Books That Focus on the Twentieth Century

On American fruit companies in Central America, see Frederick Adams, *Conquest of the Tropics* (New York, 1976); Thomas L. Karnes, *Tropical Enterprise: The Standard Fruit and Steamship Company in Latin America* (Baton Rouge, 1978); and Stacy May and Mario Plaza, *The United Fruit Company in Latin America* (Washington, D.C.., 1958).

Walker and Ariel Armony, eds., *Repression, Resistance, and Democratic Transition in Central America* (Wilmington, 2000), and Mitchell Seligson and John A. Booth, *Elections and Democracy in Central America, Revisited* (Chapel Hill, 1995).

For the perspective of a fine Latin American scholar, see Edelberto Torres-Rivas's description of Central America in its historical context in his *History and Society in Central America* (Austin, 1993). See also Torres-Rivas, *Repression and Resistance: The Struggle for Democracy in Central America* (Boulder, 1989), and Aviva Chomsky and Aldo Lauria, *Identity and Struggle at the Margins of the Nation-State: The Laboring Peoples of Central America and the Hispanic Caribbean* (Durham, N.C., 1998).

THE INTERNET

There are a number of excellent resources on Central America on the Internet. The best places to start include:

United States Department of State, Country Studies, located at: http://lcweb2.loc.gov/frd/cs/cshome.html
Central Intelligence Agency, *World Factbook,* located at: http://www.cia.gov/cia/publications/factbook/index.html
United States, Department of State, *Background Notes,* located at: http://www.state.gov/p/wha/ci/

And the best of the nongovernment sites is the Latin American Information Network Center (LANIC) located at: http://lanic.utexas.edu/

Index

About the Author

THOMAS L. PEARCY is Associate Professor of History at Slippery Rock University.

Other Titles in the Greenwood Histories of the Modern Nations
Frank W. Thackeray and John E. Findling, Series Editors

The History of Argentina
Daniel K. Lewis

The History of Australia
Frank G. Clarke

The History of the Baltic States
Kevin O'Connor

The History of Brazil
Robert M. Levine

The History of Canada
Scott W. See

The History of Chile
John L. Rector

The History of China
David C. Wright

The History of Congo
Didier Gondola

The History of Cuba
Clifford L. Staten

The History of Egypt
Glenn E. Perry

The History of France
W. Scott Haine

The History of Germany
Eleanor L. Turk

The History of Ghana
Roger S. Gocking

The History of Great Britain
Anne Baltz Rodrick

The History of Holland
Mark T. Hooker

The History of India
John McLeod

The History of Indonesia
Steven Drakeley

The History of Iran
Elton L. Daniel

The History of Iraq
Courtney Hunt

The History of Ireland
Daniel Webster Hollis III

The History of Israel
Arnold Blumberg

The History of Italy
Charles L. Killinger

The History of Japan
Louis G. Perez

The History of Korea
Djun Kil Kim

The History of Mexico
Burton Kirkwood

The History of New Zealand
Tom Brooking

The History of Nigeria
Toyin Falola

The History of Poland
M.B. Biskupski

The History of Portugal
James M. Anderson

The History of Russia
Charles E. Ziegler

The History of Serbia
John K. Cox

The History of South Africa
Roger B. Beck

The History of Spain
Peter Pierson

The History of Sweden
Byron J. Nordstrom

The History of Turkey
Douglas A. Howard

The History of Venezuela
H. Micheal Tarver and Julia C. Frederick